JUDICIAL REVIEW
AND THE
REASONABLE DOUBT TEST

Kennikat Press
National University Publications
Multi-disciplinary Studies in the Law

Advisory Editor
Honorable Rudolph J. Gerber

SANFORD BYRON GABIN

JUDICIAL REVIEW
and the
REASONABLE
DOUBT TEST

National University Publications
KENNIKAT PRESS // 1980
Port Washington, N.Y. // London

Portions of this work have appeared, in somewhat different form, in the Fall 1976 issue of the *Hastings Constitutional Law Quarterly*.

Manufactured in the United States of America

Published by
Kennikat Press Corp.
Port Washington, N.Y. / London

20795

Library of Congress Cataloging in Publication Data

Gabin, Sanford Byron, 1936–
    Judicial review and the reasonable doubt test.

    (Multidisciplinary studies in the law) (National university publications)
    Bibliography: p.
    1. Judicial review—United States.
2. Judicial process—United States. I. Title.
KF4575.G3   347'.73'12   79-18923
ISBN 0-8046-9248-3

CONTENTS

ACKNOWLEDGMENTS

My thanks go to Alpheus and Christine Mason, to whom my debt, both personal and intellectual, is enormous. *No hay palabras,* as Rosalind would say. Thanks also to Duane Lockard, for being a *mensh* when it mattered; to Raoul Berger, for setting me straight about the council of revision; and, of course, to Rosalind and the Hogartys, for sharing a saga with me.

For *Rosalind* and for my *Mother*

JUDICIAL REVIEW

AND THE

REASONABLE DOUBT TEST

Sanford Byron Gabin is an Associate Professor
of Public Affairs at the University of Houston
at Clear Lake City, Texas.

INTRODUCTION

While scholarly controversy over the proper role of the Supreme Court in American government continues unabated, recent studies tend to minimize and misunderstand, if not ignore or reject, the "reasonable doubt" test as a valid standard of judicial review. Some observers even consider it futile to search for standards by which to evaluate constitutional adjudication. To Archibald Cox, for example, the pursuit entails "an insoluble dilemma." Given "the need to perform the duty of judicial review without merely second-guessing the legislature in situations where both the wisdom and constitutionality of a statute depend upon an appraisal of the same conflicting interests," Cox concludes that there "is no rule by which a judge may know where to place the emphasis, nor any scale by which the contemporary critic can measure the balance struck."[1] The Framers, Cox flatly asserts, "provided no charter by which to measure the legitimate scope and nature of constitutional adjudication."[2] Raoul Berger suggests, however, that the scope of judicial review was intended to be limited by the reasonable doubt test, "that the Framers refused to allocate a larger role to the judges than annulment of laws that plainly went out of bounds." Taking my cue from Berger, who invites "further study of the judicial role in light of its historical origins,"[3] I propose to analyze the reasonable doubt test as a measure of the legitimate scope of judicial review.

I conclude in Chapter 1 that Alexander Hamilton's rationale for judicial review in *The Federalist*, a justification shared by other Framers who supported judicial review, follows inferentially, although not necessarily, from John Locke's rationale for government in his *Second Treatise*. Just as Locke, who rejected judicial review, had argued for the impartial resolution of private disputes in accordance with natural law by judges not parties to the dispute, so Hamilton and other Framers saw the need for impartial judges, removed from participation in law-making, to interpret a written constitution for the purpose of enforcing constitutional limitations on members of political institutions whose very participation in law-making rendered them parties to the dispute, presumptively biased, and therefore unqualified to judge with finality the constitutionality of their own behavior.

I also conclude that Marshall's justification for judicial review in *Marbury v. Madison** is not completely Hamiltonian, the standing interpretation of *Marbury*, because Marshall ignored Hamilton's more persuasive impartiality argument for judicial review. I further conclude that Hamilton and other Framers, supporters and opponents of judicial review alike, repudiated judicial policy-making (indeed, I am aware of no Framer who defended judicial policy-making), and that judicial policy-making seems to have included the judicial veto of legislation not *clearly* unconstitutional.

The scope of judicial review, as contemplated by Hamilton and as illustrated by Marshall's treatment of the first issue in *McCulloch v. Maryland*, is probably tantamount to the scope of judicial review as measured by the reasonable doubt test. Such a limitation on judicial power, confining the scope of judicial judgment to the invalidation of clearly unconstitutional acts, is a method for reconciling conflicting strains in early American constitutional thought. For if judicial review was seen by its defenders, especially Hamilton, as a means for checking unconstitutional legislative and executive power, then the reasonable doubt test may well have been seen by Hamilton and others as a means for checking what Robert Yates, and later Judge John Bannister Gibson, feared would (or had) become unbridled judicial power. If this is so, then the reasonable doubt test may be viewed as a vital mechanism for maintaining a middle ground between legislative and executive supremacy on one hand and judicial supremacy on the other.

Chapter 2 focuses on James Bradley Thayer and his defense of the reasonable doubt test in his celebrated article, "The Origin and Scope

---

*Citations to cases mentioned in the text may be found in the Table of Cases.

of the American Doctrine of Constitutional Law,"[4] published in 1893. Felix Frankfurter has called Thayer's article "the most important single essay" on American constitutional law.[5] Even Charles L. Black, one of Thayer's harshest critics, has asserted that Thayer's thesis is "the source of a river that flows right by the door of today."[6] The essay, nevertheless, has been seriously misunderstood by a host of modern scholars, among them Charles Black, Felix S. Cohen, Howard E. Dean, Paul Eidelberg, Robert G. McCloskey, Eugene V. Rostow, and Martin Shapiro. Chapter 2, therefore, presents a thorough reexamination of Thayer's thesis. Chapter 2 not only defends Thayer's thesis against scholarly attack by arguing that it is a generally persuasive definition of the legitimate dimensions of judicial judgment and is consistent with the Hamiltonian doctrine of judicial review; it also revises Thayer's thesis by arguing that the reasonable doubt test should be applied not just to all national legislation but, contrary to Thayer's prescription, to all state legislation as well.

Having contended that the reasonable doubt test, properly understood and applied, is a workable, although imperfect and not completely objective, tool in constitutional adjudication, and is probably a necessary limitation on judicial judgment if judicial review is to be compatible with its Hamiltonian intentions, I analyze, in Chapters 3, 4, and 5, leading decisions of the Supreme Court from the perspective of the reasonable doubt test. In Chapter 3, I examine the period in American constitutional history between 1895 and 1936, in which the Court regularly struck down national and state regulations of the economy, often abandoning the reasonable doubt test in favor of what Thayer called the exercise of "independent" judicial judgment—judicial policy-making at the expense of reasonable legislative judgment. In Chapter 4, I analyze famous "footnote four" of Justice Stone's opinion of the Court in the *Carolene Products* case, decided in 1938, during the Court's transition from judicial supremacy in the service of property rights to the same role under the Warren Court in the service of nonproperty rights. I conclude that the footnote, which provided much of the doctrinal support for the Warren Court's constitutional jurisprudence by implying that the reasonable doubt test could be ignored when "preferred freedoms" involving certain nonproperty rights were allegedly infringed, contained suggestions not only faulty in logic and authority but also incompatible with the Hamiltonian doctrine of judicial review. Finally, I analyze in Chapter 5 leading decisions of the Warren Court in the areas of segregation, reapportionment, and criminal procedure. (Chief Justice Warren called the leading decisions in those fields the most important made by his Court.) I conclude in Chapter 5 that judged by the reasonable doubt test, the Warren Court, like some of its predecessors, does not get passing marks.

1

THE HAMILTONIAN DOCTRINE OF
JUDICIAL REVIEW

John Locke "dominates American political thought," Louis Hartz has observed, "as no thinker anywhere dominates the political thought of a nation." Not surprisingly, however, Hartz regards judicial review as a "highly non-Lockean" institutional innovation,[1] for Locke, of course, advocated legislative supremacy. Willmoore Kendall even warns that "those seeking ammunition with which to defend America's peculiar institution will look in vain for it in the *Second Treatise.*"[2] On the contrary, the Hamiltonian rationale for judicial review can be found in Locke's political theory: it is an inferential, if unacknowledged, extension of Locke's justification for government.

Central to Locke's political theory were the "inconveniences" of his mythical state of nature, which persuade rational men to abandon that environment in favor of civil society and to establish government for the preservation of natural rights and the public good. Lacking in Locke's state of nature was, first, "an established, settled, known law," commonly agreed to be the standard of right and wrong for deciding "all controversies" between men. For, although the unwritten law of nature was "plain and intelligible to all rational creatures, yet men, being *biased by their interest,* as well as *ignorant for want of study of it,* are not apt to allow of it as a law binding to them in the application of it to their particular cases." The second inconvenience of the state of nature was the absence of "a known and *indifferent judge,* with authority to determine all differences according to the established law. For everyone in that state being both judge and executioner of the law of nature, men being *partial to themselves,* passion and revenge is very apt to carry them too far, and with too much heat in their own cases, as well as negligence and unconcernedness, make them too remiss in other men's." Finally, man in the state of nature lacked "power to back and support the sentence when right, and to give it due execution."[3]

Locke consistently objected to the partiality of men in a state of nature where everyone was "judge, interpreter, and executioner" of the unwritten law of nature. It was "unreasonable," he repeatedly insisted, "for men to be judges in their own cases," because "self-love" would make men "partial to themselves and their friends" and "ill-nature, passion and revenge" would bias men in punishing others. The inconveniences of the state of nature, Locke concluded, "must certainly be great where men may be judges in their own case, since ... he who was so unjust as to do his brother an injury, will scarce be so just as to condemn himself for it."[4]

The absence of "impartial," "indifferent," "unbiased," "disinterested" judges, which Locke considered absolutely necessary for the settlement of disputes in accordance with natural law, condemned the state of nature and justified—probably necessitated—government. The end of civil society, for Locke, was "to avoid and remedy those inconveniences of the state of nature which necessarily follow from every man's being judge in his own case." "Government," Locke continually emphasized, "is to be the remedy of those evils, which necessarily follow from men's being judges in their own cases."[5]

Locke's system of government, therefore, required that "whoever has the legislative or supreme power ... is bound to govern by established standing laws, promulgated and known to the people, ... by indifferent and upright judges, who are to decide controversies by those laws." Such an arrangement, intended to resolve disputes peacefully and impartially in accordance with natural law, "puts men out of a state of nature." Indeed, any political system which fails in this purpose is, in effect, a continuation of the state of nature.[6]

Yet Locke's remedy for the inconveniences of the state of nature was by his own admission necessarily imperfect, for it could not preclude the possibility of governmental tyranny or the consequent possibility of popular revolution. Posed toward the end of his *Second Treatise* is "the old question," "the common question": when the people's chosen representatives are alleged to have violated the trust imposed by the social compact or the limits imposed by natural law, who is to judge the transgression? Locke's response, considered especially with his rationale for government, provides support for judicial review of limited scope. Locke, of course, placed ultimate judgment with the people to determine and to redress governmental violations of the social compact and natural law. Thus "the community perpetually retains a supreme power of saving themselves from the attempts and designs of anybody, even of their legislators, wherever they shall be so foolish or so wicked as to lay and carry on designs against the liberties and properties of the subject." "There remains still in the people a supreme power to remove or alter the legislative, when they find the legislative act contrary to the trust reposed in them."[7] Furthermore, community determination of both the legitimacy of governmental behavior as well as the right to rebel meant, for Locke, decision by the numerical majority. Ultimately, then, the definition and protection of natural rights rested with a government responsible to the majority.[8]

Locke's own premises, however, required impartial resolution of disputes which necessitated unbiased judges not parties to the dispute. Yet this condition is clearly absent when either the political branches of government or the community at large attempts to judge alleged violations of the social compact or natural law. Both bodies are, by Locke's definition, parties to the dispute, the legislative and executive branches having made and enforced the challenged law and the majority of the people having no special claim to impartiality especially with respect to the interests of aggrieved minorities.[9]

Locke himself even seemed to recognize the difficulty of reconciling majoritarian government with natural law limitations on government when an impartial, accurate determination of those limitations was exceedingly hard to make. Accordingly, he suggested two significant restraints on the exercise of popular, majoritarian judgment of alleged governmental violations of natural law: only in the absence of "a judicature on earth to decide" and only "in a matter where the law is silent or doubtful, and the thing be of great consequence." That Locke several times confined popular judgment and redress of alleged governmental tyranny to cases "where there lies no appeal on earth" or which admit of "no appeal to a judge on earth"[10] surely permits, without requiring, the inference that an institution capable of judging such controversies impartially might constitute an improvement on his political system. Finally, Locke's limitation of popular judgment to cases where natural law is "silent or doubtful" would correspondingly seem to limit the permissible scope of judicial judgment, should judicial review be established, to clear, unambiguous violations of natural law; for where natural law is silent or ambiguous, even impartial judicial judgment is, by definition, mere choice between constitutionally permissible alternatives. Preference between alternatives not clearly precluded by higher law would, therefore, be made by the political branches which were ultimately responsible to the people. Perhaps unwittingly, John Locke had laid potentially sound theoretical foundations for judicial review, an institution which played absolutely no part in the Englishman's own political system.

Relevant American constitutional thought precedes the establishment of judicial review and John Marshall's justification. Refusal by the Philadelphia convention to associate the Judiciary with the Executive in a council of revision that would have been empowered to review the wisdom of proposed legislation was grounded in the conviction that judicial impartiality required separation of the judicial function from the legislative process. While Marshall's later assertion of judicial review might have been taken for granted, even invited, by the Framers,[11] they drew a sharp distinction between judicial interpretation of the Constitution with finality and judicial policy-making. "There is a difference," John Dickinson of Delaware insisted. "The judges must interpret the laws; they ought not to be legislators." "It was," Elbridge Gerry of Massachusetts agreed, "quite foreign from the nature of the office to make them judges of the policy of public measures." The separation of powers principle emphatically precluded, as Gerry put it, "making Statesmen of the Judges."[12]

Furthermore, judges were not considered especially qualified as policy-makers. "A knowledge of mankind and of legislative affairs," Luther Martin of Maryland counseled, "cannot be presumed to belong in a higher degree to the Judges than to the Legislature." "As Judges," Nathaniel Gorham of Massachusetts observed, "they are not to be presumed to possess any peculiar knowledge of the mere policy of public measures." John Rutledge of South Carolina, soon to become a charter member of the Supreme Court and later its second Chief Justice, even "thought the Judges of all men the most unfit to be concerned in the Revisionary Council."[13]

Separation of powers, at least with respect to determination of policy by legislators and of constitutionality by judges, was not based, however, on a blind faith in judges qua judges, peculiarly endowed as infallible interpreters of the Constitution. Rather, the principle rested on the assumption that the Judiciary, if kept independent and neutral, would more likely be a faithful, impartial expounder of the document than would either the Legislature or the Executive. Accordingly, Gouverneur Morris of Pennsylvania scored "the impropriety of being Judge in one's own cause." Gorham warned that "the Judges ought to carry into the exposition of the laws no prepossessions with regard to them." Rufus King of Massachusetts urged that they should be able to expound the law "free from the bias of having participated in its formation."[14] It followed that associating the Judiciary with the Executive in a legislative revisionary capacity would adversely affect the impartiality of the judges when later called upon to decide issues of constitutionality. "The Judges in exercising the function of expositors," Caleb Strong of Massachusetts feared, "might be influenced by the part they had taken in framing the laws." Charles Pinckney of South Carolina also "opposed the interference of the Judges in the Legislative business; it will involve them in parties, and give a previous tincture to their opinions."[15]

Although the Framers unequivocally rejected judicial policy-making in a council of revision, the convention sheds less light on whether they then recognized that judicial policy-making might be invited by interpretation with finality of an often silent, ambiguous Constitution. While none of the delegates endorsed judicial policy-making, Dickinson alone expressed the fear that the Judiciary, even without a formal revisionary power, might exert a legislative influence. The "Justiciary of Aragon," he recalled, "became by degrees the law giver."[16]

Subdued or generally ignored at Philadelphia, this issue, the legitimate scope of judicial review, did not pass unnoticed in the ratification debates. Antifederalist opposition to the Constitution, aimed primarily at allegedly excessive national power and at the absence of a bill of rights, exposed the potential implications of judicial review. Robert Yates, who departed the convention when its nationalist direction seemed to him irreversible and became an eloquent critic of the proposed constitution, foresaw in the combination of judicial review and the intended nature of the document itself the promise of both national and judicial supremacy. "Most of the articles in this system, which convey powers of any considerable importance," the New Yorker observed, "are conceived in general and indefinite terms, which are either equivocal, ambiguous, or which require long definitions to unfold the extent of their meaning." "A number of hard words and technical phrases are used," Yates noted, "about the meaning of which gentlemen learned in the law differ."[17]

Nationalists and Antifederalists alike agreed with Yates's description of the Constitution. "So loosely, so inaccurately" were national powers defined, John Smilie of Pennsylvania believed, that "it will be impossible" without "a full and explicit declaration of rights" to "ascertain the limits of authority, and to declare when government has degenerated into oppression."[18] Without more precise definition, William Bodman of Massachusetts argued, the national powers enumerated in Article 1, Section 8, were "certainly unlimited, and therefore dangerous." John Williams of New York conceded that it was probably "utterly impossible fully to define" the broad discretionary powers latent in the Necessary and Proper Clause. Likewise, he asked, "are not the terms *common defence* and *general welfare* indefinite, undefinable terms?" Antifederalists searched vainly for a constitutional line clearly limiting national power in relation to the states and the people. "It was of the highest importance," Melancton Smith of New York urged, "that the line of jurisdiction should be accurately drawn."[19]

But Antifederalist insistence that national power be precisely defined met with stubborn refusal. "Is it, indeed, possible," Jasper Yeates of Pennsylvania wondered, "to define any power so accurately, that it shall reach the particular object for which it was given, and yet not be liable to perversion and abuse?" James Wilson of Pennsylvania, undeviating advocate of indefinite, undefined national power, would not pretend "that the line is drawn with mathematical precision; the inaccuracy of language must, to a certain degree, prevent the accomplishment of such a desire."[20] Consistently with the position he and James Madison had taken in the Philadelphia convention,[21] Wilson declared flatly that national power should not be limited.[22]

Not just the imperfection of language[23] contributed to an inaccurate definition of national power; nationalists had clearly intended its indefinite, undefined scope. Join judicial review with a document of *that* nature, Robert Yates feared, and the Judiciary would be able "to mould the government into almost any shape they please." The judges had been empowered "not only to carry into execution the powers expressly given, but where these are wanting or ambiguously expressed, to supply what is wanting by their own decisions." "They will," he went on, "give the sense of every article of the constitution, that may from time to time come before them. And in their decisions they will not confine themselves to any fixed or established rules, but will determine, according to what appears to them, the reason and spirit of the constitution." Such power, Yates emphasized, transcended any before given a judiciary "by any free government under heaven." The judges had been made independent "in the fullest sense of the word. . . . In short, they are independent of the people, of the legislature, and of every power under heaven. Men placed in this situation will generally soon feel themselves independent of heaven itself." Concluding his critique, Yates came out for the Lockean alternative, legislative supremacy:

> Had the construction of the constitution been left with the legislature, they would have explained it at their peril; if they exceed their powers, or sought to find, in the spirit of the constitution, more than was expressed in the letter, the people from whom they derived their power could remove them, and do themselves right; and indeed I can see no other remedy that the people can have against their rulers for encroachments of this nature. A constitution is a compact of a people with their rulers; if the rulers break the compact, the people have a right and ought to remove them, and do themselves justice; but in order to enable them to do this with the greater facility, those whom the people choose at stated periods should have the power in the last resort to determine the sense of the compact; if they determine contrary to the understanding of the people, an appeal will lie to the people at the period when the rulers are to be elected, and they will have it in their power to remedy the evil; but when this power is lodged in the hands of men independent of the people, and of their representatives, and who are not, constitutionally, accountable for their opinions, no way is left to control them but *with a high hand and an outstretched arm.*[24]

So powerful was Yates's attack on the potential judicial supremacy inherent, he thought, in the proposed system of government that Alexander Hamilton replied specifically to him in *The Federalist.* In their premises as well as their arguments Yates and Hamilton were poles apart. Yates opposed judicial review because judicial independence, he believed, would free the Judiciary to manipulate legislatively an ambiguous constitution; far from securing impartiality, judicial independence, coupled with an ambiguous document, permitted, even encouraged, judicial bias. To Hamilton independence cut precisely the opposite way; separation of the Judiciary from the political branches and from the people, the indispensable premise in his justification of judicial review, would free the Judiciary to interpret the Constitution impartially.

Hamilton's rationale, later followed incompletely by Marshall, does not depend, however, on "magic," an "act of creation," an "act of prestidigitation." It does, of course, reflect a faith, perhaps unjustified, in independent judges, but it does not invoke a "miracle."[25] Instead, Hamilton reasoned, the judicial power must be committed "not to a part of the legislature" but to a "distinct and independent" department,[26] because "no man ought certainly to be a judge in his own cause, or in any cause in respect to which he has the least interest or bias."[27] "From a body which had even a partial agency in passing bad laws," Hamilton explained, "we could rarely expect a disposition to temper and moderate [those laws] in the application. The same spirit which had operated in making them would be too apt in interpreting them; *still less could it be expected that men who had infringed the Constitution in the character of legislators would be disposed to repair the breach in the character of judges.*" To be sure, Hamilton believed that judges would more likely be "selected for their knowledge of the laws, acquired by long and laborious study," than would legislators; but legislators, even if learned in the law, would be biased because of their "natural propensity" to "party divisions." "The habit of being continually marshalled on opposite sides," he thought, "will be too apt to stifle the voice both of law and equity."[28]

While Hamilton argued the likelihood of legislative incompetence in the task of judging, he did not assume judicial infallibility. Indeed, the possibility of judicial error, even bias, forced Hamilton to concede that judicial fallibility required a limitation on the scope of judicial judgment. "There are endless diversities in the opinions of men," he observed. "We often see not only different courts but the judges of the same court differing from each other."[29] "Particular misconstructions and contraventions of the will of the legislature may now and then happen," Hamilton admitted; "but they can never be so extensive," he thought, "as to amount to an inconvenience, or in any sensible degree to affect the order of the political system."[30] Nevertheless, Hamilton warned, the improper "exercise of judicial discretion" would transform judicial review into judicial supremacy. Invalidation of legislation on the mere "pretence of a repugnancy" to the Constitution would amount to the substitution of judicial policy-making for "the constitutional intentions of the legislature." If, moreover, judges "should be disposed to exercise WILL instead of JUDGMENT, the consequence would equally be the substitution of their pleasure to that of the legislative body. *The observation, if it prove anything, would prove that there ought to be no judges independent of that body.*"[31] Violation of the legitimate *scope* of judicial review, Hamilton confessed, would destroy its *rationale.* If, as Yates feared, the independence of judges freed them to exercise biased judgment, then the Hamiltonian justification of judicial review would expire, for it extended only to the exercise of impartial judgment—which, Hamilton argued, required an independent judiciary.

Impressive in answering the question *who* judges and *why,* and perceptive in linking the legitimacy of judicial review to its proper scope, Hamilton is less satisfactory in defining that scope. Rejected by the Philadelphia convention was, of course, judicial review of the wisdom of legislation.[32] Fashioning and executing "wise" or "good" public policy— the very essence of statesmanship, the politician's most exalted function— was intentionally conferred on the political branches alone. Hamilton agreed and therefore proscribed the exercise of judicial *will.* But how does one distinguish *judgment* from *will? What kind* of judgment and *how much* is legitimate? How much judicial discretion in construing an often ambiguous constitution is permissible? "To avoid an arbitrary discretion in the courts," Hamilton declared, "it is indispensable that they should be bound down by strict rules and precedents, which serve to define and point out their duty in every particular case that comes before them." But what constitutes "arbitrary" discretion, and what kind of "rules" of constitutional construction should judges employ to avoid arbitrary discretion? Hamilton answered, somewhat helpfully, that the judicial duty to void legislation contrary to "the manifest tenor" of the Constitution arises only if "an irreconcilable variance" exists between the Constitution and the challenged enactment, implying that in doubtful cases judges should withhold their veto. Hamilton did not, however, elaborate on the problems implicit in "the faithful performance of so arduous a duty."[33]

Despite Hamilton's incomplete treatment of the proper limits of judicial judgment, his justification of judicial review in *The Federalist* seems far more persuasive than John Marshall's in *Marbury v. Madison* (1803). Marshall's rationale, notwithstanding prevailing opinion to the contrary, is *not* "thoroughly Hamiltonian in assuming that only judges can know the Constitution or will base their interpretation of it on knowledge rather than will."[34] Hamilton had argued from the need for impartial and therefore independent judges, a requirement which militated against final constitutional interpretation by the political branches. But judges were not presumed infallible. Although theoretically barred from the exercise of will and believed more likely than members of the political branches to construe the Constitution impartially, judges, Hamilton realized, were capable of exercising will instead of judgment. Violations of the judicial function, "usurpations," "encroachments on the legislative authority" were possible, Hamilton thought, and deserved to be curbed.[35] Marshall's rationale for judicial review, unlike Hamilton's, simply begged the question. Marshall blithely jumped to the conclusion that judicial review was the "very essence of judicial duty" and offered the least compelling of reasons, which included neither the infallibility argument, wrongly attributed to him and to Hamilton, nor the impartiality argument, the core of Hamilton's justification.

"The question," Marshall confidently began in *Marbury*, "whether an act repugnant to the Constitution, can become the law of the land, is a question deeply interesting to the United States; but, happily, not of an intricacy proportioned to its interest." Marshall's assurance of easily resolving the interesting-but-not-intricate issue is understandable; he had already sidestepped the real question, which was not whether an act repugnant to the Constitution could stand, but who should decide whether the act is unconstitutional. Positing the limited nature of the government established by the Constitution, Marshall derived "a proposition too plain to be contested": the Constitution is a paramount law to which ordinary legislative acts must conform. It followed that a legislative act contrary to the Constitution is not law and must not be given effect in court; otherwise "written constitutions are absurd attempts, on the part of the people, to limit a power in its own nature illimitable."

Whereas Hamilton had offered credible reasons for empowering the Judiciary to decide when paramount law conflicted with inferior law, Marshall neatly avoided the issue. He came closest to confronting it when he declared that the *absence* of judicial review "would subvert the very foundation of all written constitutions." It would mean, Marshall asserted, "that an Act which, according to the principles and theory of our government, is entirely void, is yet, in practice, completely obligatory. It would declare that if the legislature shall do what is expressly forbidden, such Act, notwithstanding the express prohibition, is in reality effectual. It would be giving to the legislature a practical and real omnipotence, with the same breath which professes to restrict their powers within narrow limits. It is prescribing limits, and declaring that those limits may be passed at pleasure."

Yet even in this passage Marshall's logic is incomplete. He seemed to assume—correctly—that the absence of judicial review would leave final construction of the Constitution to the political branches and ultimately the people, but Marshall failed, unlike Hamilton, to demonstrate *why* this result is *undesirable* and *why* judicial review is *preferable*. For it does not follow—*without reasons*—that the legislature would ignore constitutional limitations, and it does not follow—*without reasons*—that the Judiciary would be more likely than the political branches to interpret the Constitution faithfully. Nevertheless, Marshall arbitrarily concluded that the absence of judicial review would *necessarily* mean the absence of constitutional limitations on the political branches. That result, he tautologically urged, would be absurd, given a written constitution intended to limit political power; but he did not argue, as Hamilton had, the absurdity of allowing those whose power is supposed to be limited to interpret with finality the document limiting their own power.[36] Nor did Marshall assert, as Hamilton had, that judges, being detached from and independent of the political arena as well as trained in the law, would be better suited as impartial interpreters of the Constitution than would legislators—who, no matter how well informed in the law, would have their independence and therefore their ability to judge impartially impaired by their necessary dependence on politics and on the people. Finally, unlike Hamilton, Marshall in *Marbury* neither alleged nor denied judicial infallibility. Although Marshall's opinion is "justly celebrated," as Robert G. McCloskey has written, "not the least of its virtues is the fact that it is somewhat beside the point."[37] "It will not bear scrutiny," Learned Hand succinctly stated.[38]

John Bannister Gibson, foremost contemporary critic of Marshall's justification of judicial review, agreed. His dissenting opinion in *Eakin v. Raub*, an otherwise insignificant case decided by the Pennsylvania Supreme Court in 1825, has been dubbed by James Bradley Thayer "much the ablest discussion of the question which I have ever seen, not excepting the judgment of Marshall in *Marbury v. Madison*, which as I venture to think has been overpraised."[39] So too has Gibson's critique of judicial review been overpraised. His attack on Marshall's rationale, while generally impressive, overlooks what Marshall himself ignored—Hamilton's more persuasive justification. Moreover, Gibson's defense of the Lockean alternative is not itself impeccable.

Gibson's argument has five main thrusts: it emphasizes the absence of an express constitutional grant of final reviewing power to the Judiciary;

it urges that the Constitution precludes any inference of judicial review it asserts that the legislature is peculiarly able to judge the constitutionality of its own behavior and further that legislative supremacy is the only institutional arrangement compatible with American constitutional thought; it spurns judicial review as an unnecessary and ineffective device for enforcing written constitutions; and it implies that judicial review inevitably means the exercise of judicial will.

In what part of the Constitution, Gibson asked, are we to look for "this proud pre-eminence?" Had judicial review been clearly intended, it would have been placed on "the impregnable ground of an express grant." Lacking that, it could be supported only by "irresistible implication" from the document itself. But the Constitution did not imply judicial review. In fact, the oath provision furnished "an argument equally plausible against the right of the judiciary."[40] Moreover, the foundation of every argument in favor of judicial review, Gibson concluded, "is found at last to be an assumption of the whole ground in dispute."

Gibson conceded that an act of the legislature, were it to conflict with the Constitution, "a law of superior obligation," would have to fall. "But it is a fallacy," he insisted, "to suppose that they can come into collision before the judiciary." Thus, Gibson contended not only that judicial review was not *necessarily* implied by the Constitution but more significantly that it was an *impermissible* inference. Legislative supremacy alone, he claimed, was consistent with the theory of government embodied in the Constitution. Rejecting the notion that the three branches of the national government were coequal, Gibson, following Locke, declared that "the legislative organ is superior to every other, inasmuch as the power to will and command is essentially superior to the power to act and obey." It does not follow, Gibson thought, "that every organ created by special provision in the constitution is of equal rank." Indeed, "the executive, strictly as such, and the judiciary are subordinate; and an act of superior power exercised by an inferior ought, one would think, rest on something more solid than implication."

Gibson's argument for legislative supremacy does not stand up. The legislature is deemed "superior" because the power to "will and command" is superior to the power to "act and obey." But the Constitution *limits* legislative power; the question of who should interpret and enforce those limits cannot be settled by reference to legislative superiority any more satisfactorily than Marshall's assertion of judicial review can be justified by reliance *alone* on a written constitution limiting government.

Other reasons must be advanced, and they do *not* include Gibson's unwarranted assumption that the rationale for judicial review presupposes coequal branches of the national government.

Gibson, however, did offer other reasons. Apparently rejecting Hamilton's requirement of impartial judges, Gibson insisted that legislators were better qualified than independent judges to interpret the Constitution. Each branch of the government, he thought, "must be supposed to have a superior capacity only for those things which peculiarly belong to it;" and, he continued, "as legislation peculiarly involves the consideration of those limitations which are put on the law-making power, and the interpretation of the laws when made involves only the construction of the laws themselves, it follows that the construction of the Constitution in this particular belongs to the legislature, which ought therefore to be taken to have superior capacity to judge of the constitutionality of its own acts." With this assertion the crucial issue seems, at last, joined. But Gibson went no further, and his mere claim of inherent legislative superiority in construing the Constitution partakes of the same arbitrariness involved in the counterclaim, often erroneously imputed to Hamilton, that judges, simply because they are learned in the law, are better able than anyone else to interpret the document with finality. Thus, Gibson neither acknowledged nor disposed of Hamilton's specific and reasoned denial of the contention that the legislature has a "superior capacity to judge of the constitutionality of its own acts." For Hamilton, as for the other Framers who spoke to the issue, accurate constitutional construction demanded impartiality as well as knowledge; it was, therefore, peculiarly inappropriate to be a judge in one's own cause.

Gibson's preference for legislative supremacy went hand in hand with his profound distrust of judicial review and of written constitutions. Although conceding that a written constitution was "an instrument of inestimable value . . . in rendering its principles familiar to the mass of the people," he warned that "there is no magic or inherent power in parchment and ink to command respect and protect principles from violation." Ultimately, Gibson insisted, "there is no effectual guard against legislative usurpation but public opinion, the force of which, in this country, is inconceivably great." Furthermore, public opinion was "a sufficient guard against palpable infractions."

Given this bias, judicial review was unnecessary. Rather, Gibson, like Locke and Yates, believed that "it rests with the people, in whom full and sovereign power resides, to correct abuses in legislation, by instructing their representatives to repeal the obnoxious Act." It was "a postulate in the theory of our government, and the very basis of the super-structure," he declared, "that the people are wise, virtuous, and competent to manage their own affairs." The political process, then, was the only proper check on unconstitutional legislation. To add judicial review, Gibson thought, would unnecessarily impair the energy of government, already dangerously weakened by a bevy of checks and balances. "The notion of a complication of counterchecks," he lamented, "has been carried to an extent in theory, of which the framers of the Constitution never dreamt."

Gibson's reliance on American constitutional thought to support legislative supremacy leaves much to be desired. He ignored some fundamental propositions that contradict his interpretation of "the theory of our government." The Framers, to be sure, had a certain amount of faith in the people, but they were not deemed so "wise, virtuous, and competent" as to render unnecessary the checks and balances the Constitution embodies. Indeed, Antifederalists viewed the proposed constitution as having *too few* checks and balances, so little faith had they in human nature and especially in people occupying positions of political power.[41] Even such staunch nationalists as Hamilton and Madison had a mixed view of human nature.[42]

Furthermore, Gibson's claim that the people, through what he considered an overly complicated political process, were intended to be the sole check on unconstitutional legislation finds little or no support in the record.[43] On unwise legislation, yes; on unconstitutional legislation, no. "A dependence on the people," James Madison commented in a frequently quoted passage in *The Federalist,* "is, no doubt, the *primary control* on the government; but experience has taught mankind the necessity of *auxiliary precautions.*"[44] Madison himself, once converted by Thomas Jefferson concerning the need for a bill of rights, argued strenuously for judicial review as an essential "auxiliary precaution" against invasion of individual rights.[45] "If they are incorporated into the Constitution," Madison proclaimed when proposing the Bill of Rights amendments to the House of Representatives in 1789, "independent tribunals of justice will consider themselves in a peculiar manner the guardians of those rights; they will be an impenetrable bulwark against every assumption of power in the legislative or executive; they will be naturally led to resist every encroachment upon rights *expressly* stipulated for in the constitution by the declaration of rights."[46]

Even Gibson, curiously and surprisingly, conceded that there might be rare occasions justifying—indeed, necessitating—the use of judicial power to resist governmental tyranny. Such "monstrous violations of the Constitution," he admitted,

> as taking away the trial by jury, the elective franchise, or subverting religious liberty ... would be such a usurpation of the political rights of the citizens, as would work a change in the very structure of the government; or, to speak more properly, it would itself be a revolution, which, to counteract, would justify even insurrection; consequently, a judge might lawfully employ every instrument of official resistance within his reach. By this I mean, that while the citizen should resist with pike and gun, the judge might co-operate with *habeas corpus* and *mandamus*. It would be his duty, as a citizen, to throw himself into the breach, and, if it should be necessary, perish there; but this is far from proving the judiciary to be a peculiar organ under the Constitution to prevent legislative encroachment on the powers reserved by the people; and this is all I contend it is not.[47]

This is a most significant, most unusual passage, especially considered in light of "the theory of our government" that Gibson invoked in support of legislative supremacy. Gibson, paradoxically, did not think of judicial review as a legitimate means of avoiding revolution; rather he advocated the use of other forms of judicial power to assist justified counter-revolution against clear and extreme forms of governmental tyranny. Many of the Framers would probably have likened Gibson's view of the proper exercise of judicial power to locking the barn door after the horse had been stolen. Moreover, some of the Framers, including Madison and Hamilton, clearly advocated judicial review, particularly of legislation violating the Bill of Rights, primarily to avoid recourse to revolution by aggrieved citizens.[48] Gibson, then, ignored what leading Framers considered a special and compelling argument for judicial review and what leading scholars have since considered America's greatest improvement over the "yawning hiatus"[49] in Locke's system.

Gibson's final quarrel with judicial review concerned the fallibility of judges. The exercise of judicial judgment, he believed, meant the likely exercise of judicial will, which he considered more difficult to check than legislative violations of the Constitution. Yet Gibson, whose entire case against judicial review seems ambivalent,[50] conceded that "it might, perhaps, have been better to vest the power in the judiciary; as it might be expected that its habits of deliberation, and the aid derived from the arguments of counsel, would more frequently lead to accurate conclusions."[51] "On the other hand," he added, second thoughts apparently prevailing, "the judiciary is not infallible; and an error by it would admit of no remedy but a more distinct expression of the public will, through the extraordinary medium of a convention; whereas, an error by the legislature admits of a remedy by an exertion of the same will, in the ordinary exercise of the right of suffrage—a mode better calculated to attain the end without popular excitement."

To the claim that the exercise of judicial review was "restricted to cases that are free from doubt or difficulty," Gibson replied that repugnance to the Constitution is not always "self-evident." "To say, therefore, that the power is to be exercised but in perfectly clear cases," he concluded, "is to betray a doubt of the propriety of exercising it at all." Gibson's attack on what he viewed as an unbridled scope for judicial judgment had been invited, of course, by Marshall's awkward application of judicial review in *Marbury*, where the examples the Chief Justice cited as appropriate for exercise of the judicial veto are all clear and unambiguous provisions of the Constitution. Yet Marshall's own interpretation of Section 13 of the Judiciary Act of 1789, which he deemed an unconstitutional attempt to expand the Court's original jursidiction, was itself an embarrassing counterexample, where repugnance to the Constitution was not self-evident.[52]

However, before we accept Gibson's indictment of Marshall for failing to delimit the legitimate dimensions of judicial judgment, it will be profitable to look beyond *Marbury* to *McCulloch v. Maryland* (1819), in which Marshall applied judicial standards compatible with Hamilton's rationale for judicial review, effectively refuting the contention of Yates and Gibson that judicial review, given the fallibility of judges and the often ambiguous nature of the Constitution, necessarily implied the exercise of judicial will. Unlike the examples cited in *Marbury*, the first constitutional issue in *McCulloch*—whether Congress had the power to incorporate a national bank—involved interpretation of a constitutional ambiguity; for the Constitution did not expressly confer or deny that power, and the Necessary and Proper Clause bore conflicting meanings, one supporting and the other precluding the necessity of the bank. Why, then, did Marshall uphold the power of Congress to establish the bank? Consider Edward S. Corwin's explanation, attributing Marshall's decision solely to the exercise of judicial will:

The truth is that the major premise of most of the great decisions of the Supreme Court is a concealed bias of some sort—a highly laudable bias, perhaps, yet a bias. For example, the question at issue in *McCullough [sic] v. Maryland* was the meaning of the phrase "necessary and proper"; did it mean "absolutely necessary" or "convenient"? Marshall said it meant "convenient." But why, except that he was a nationalist? Now, however, suppose he had decided that the phrase in question had borne the other meaning. His particularistic bias would have resulted in the overthrow of the will of the Federal legislature. Or to put the whole matter in a sentence: the real question at issue when the validity of an act of Congress is challenged before the Supreme Court is *not* whether the fundamental Constitution shall give way to an act of Congress, but whether Congress' interpretation of the fundamental Constitution shall prevail or whether it shall yield to that of another human, and therefore presumably fallible, institution—a bench of judges.[53]

Corwin also insisted that Marshall's famous statement in *McCulloch*— "we must never forget that it is *a constitution* we are expounding . . . intended to endure for ages to come, and, consequently, to be adapted to the various *crises* of human affairs"[54] —implied the need for *judicial* policy-making, for the statesmanlike exercise of *judicial* will, in short, a *judicial* duty to adapt the Constitution, thereby rendering it a living charter capable of growth.[55] Not so. For Marshall, at least in *McCulloch*, it was the duty of the *political* branches, not the Judiciary, to adapt the "great outlines" of the Constitution to the changing needs of society; consequently, it was the duty of the Judiciary to uphold constitutionally permissible *legislative* will.

In deciding, therefore, whether Congress could establish a national bank, Marshall observed that the "great powers" of Congress—to lay and collect taxes; to borrow money; to regulate commerce; to declare and conduct a war; and to raise and support armies and navies—were, although enumerated, obviously undefined and hence susceptible of broad construction. Moreover, because the Constitution did not specifically prohibit the creation of a corporation by Congress or "enumerate the means by which the powers it confers may be executed," the Court had to inquire "how far such means may be employed." Only "necessary and proper" means could be used, but this phrase had a variety of meanings, including both the restrictive interpretation ("absolutely necessary" or "indispensable") and the permissive interpretation ("convenient"). Each was a rational, plausible interpretation. "A thing," Marshall indicated, "may be necessary, very necessary, absolutely or indispensably necessary. To no mind would the same idea be conveyed, by these several phrases." Congress and the President thought the means necessary, and, Marshall emphasized, it "would require no ordinary share of intrepidity to assert that [their judgment] was *a bold and plain usurpation,* to which the constitution gave no countenance."[56] Constitutional ambiguity required judicial deference to reasonable legislative interpretation, Marshall made eminently clear in a memorable, if usually misunderstood, passage:

> The subject is the execution of those great powers on which the welfare of a nation essentially depends. It must have been the intention of those who gave these powers, to insure, as far as human prudence could insure, their beneficial execution. This could not be done by confiding [sic] the choice of means to such narrow limits as not to leave it *in the power of Congress* to adopt any which might be appropriate and which were conducive to the end. *This provision is made in a constitution intended to endure for ages to come, and, consequently, to be adapted to the various crises of human affairs.* To have prescribed the means by which government should, in all future time, execute its powers, would have been to change, entirely, the character of the instrument, and give it the properties of a legal code. It would have been an unwise attempt to provide, by immutable rules, for exigencies which, if foreseen at all, must have been seen dimly, and which can be best provided for as they occur. To have declared that the best means shall not be used, but those alone without which the power given would be nugatory, would have been to deprive *the legislature* of the capacity to avail itself of experience, to exercise *its reason,* and to accommodate *its legislation* to circumstances.[57]

Constitutional creativity, then, was a political, not a judicial, prerogative; for "to inquire into the degree of [the law's] necessity, would be to pass the line which circumscribes the judicial department, and to tread on legislative ground." "This court," Marshall asserted, "disclaims all pretensions to such a power."

Yates's prediction that where constitutional powers had been "ambiguously expressed" the Judiciary would necessarily "supply what is wanting by their own decisions" had been unfounded. Marshall's impartiality in *McCulloch* precluded the exercise of judicial will and was therefore consistent with the Hamiltonian rationale for judicial review. Ironically, final construction of the Constitution, where ambiguity permitted differing rational interpretations, had properly been left where Locke, Yates, and Gibson preferred—with the political branches and ultimately the people. Nevertheless, Gibson's tart inference—that limiting the exercise of the judicial veto to "cases that are free from doubt" betrayed "a doubt of the propriety of exercising it at all"—was patently incorrect. For the mere fact of constitutional ambiguity did not preclude the need for impartial judgment on the very issues of ambiguity and of reasonable legislative construction. The judicial veto would still be properly invoked when the legislature clearly misinterpreted the scope of its power.

Whereas "the necessity of the case" finally led Gibson to embrace judicial review,[58] Hamilton had reached the same conclusion much earlier. He made the logical leap John Locke's own premises had permitted but which Locke himself had refused to take. For Hamilton's rationale for judicial review rested on the Lockean justification for government, the very argument which prompted the Philadelphia convention to refuse to associate the Judiciary with a council of revision. Just as Locke deplored being a judge in one's own cause, just as the convention disapproved of judges determining the constitutionality of legislation they had helped to frame, so did Hamilton frown on the political branches judging with finality the constitutionality of legislation they had enacted.

Hamilton's justification, moreover, neither proceeded from nor depended on a blind faith in the infallibility of judges. Rather, it rested on a reasoned belief in independence from political involvement as essential for "the faithful performance of so arduous a duty": impartial judgment of the constitutionality of political conduct. Perhaps the long view—history—will persuade some that the belief was misplaced, that just as Locke was unreasonable "only in his faith in reason,"[59] in the reasonableness of popular majorities not subject to judicial review, so Hamilton was unreasonable only in his faith in independent judges. Nevertheless, the belief was not without rational foundation, given the Hamiltonian premium on independence as a prerequisite for the goal of impartial judicial judgment.

Nor was Hamilton's rationale faithfully followed by Marshall in *Marbury,* for judicial review does not necessarily emerge either from the fact of a written constitution limiting government or from the constitutional text. Hamilton, eschewing the text, advanced reasons for judicial review which Marshall in *Marbury* overlooked or ignored,[60] thus exposing his logic to the criticism of Gibson and a host of modern scholars. Gibson's attack on judicial review, then, was aimed at the wrong man. He never really faced up to Hamilton's argument, even when he seemed to acknowledge the issue.

Hamilton's main contribution to the search for standards by which to judge judges is found, therefore, in his answer to *who* judges and *why?* Marshall's contribution, on the other hand, is found not in *Marbury* but in *McCulloch,* where he furthered the quest for the permissible dimensions of judicial judgment: *what kind* of judgment and *how much* is allowable, given the Hamiltonian rationale for judicial review, the fallibility of judges, and the often ambiguous nature of the Constitution.

2

JAMES BRADLEY THAYER AND THE DIMENSIONS OF JUDICIAL JUDGMENT:
The Reasonable Doubt Test versus Independent Judgment

Hamilton in *The Federalist* and Marshall in *McCulloch v. Maryland* had provided firm foundations for a coherent doctrine of judicial review. It remained for James Bradley Thayer to rationalize further the legitimate dimensions of judicial judgment. Professor of Law at Harvard University from 1874 until his death in 1902, Thayer published in 1893 a seminal article, "The Origin and Scope of the American Doctrine of Constitutional Law."[1] A major attempt to define the proper scope of judicial review, the essay influenced such judges as Oliver Wendell Holmes, Jr., Louis D. Brandeis, Learned and Augustus Hand, and Felix Frankfurter. Indeed, Frankfurter has stated that if he had to choose only one piece of writing on American constitutional law, he would pick Thayer's article, which Frankfurter called "the most important single essay," "the great guide for judges and, therefore, the great guide for understanding by non-judges of what the place of the judiciary is in relation to constitutional questions."[2]

The essay, nevertheless, has been largely misunderstood; recurrent attacks on Thayer's thesis have obscured more than clarified his contribution to American constitutional thought. One continuing criticism has been that Thayer's "rule of administration"—his prescription that the judicial veto of legislation should be confined to clear violations of the Constitution, cases in which the challenged statute is unconstitutional "beyond a reasonable doubt"—is "radically incompatible" with democratic theory, which instead requires judicial policy-making even when the alleged invalidity of a legislative act is manifestly uncertain.[3] Critics also assert that Thayer's rule amounts to an abdication of judicial review;[4] that the mere passage of an act by presumably rational legislators would satisfy the reasonable doubt test;[5] that the distinction between clear and unclear violations of the Constitution is fatuous;[6] that Thayer's rule taken seriously would require judges to employ a sanity test to determine the rationality of legislative judgment;[7] that the rule will not resolve the problem of conflicting constitutional values;[8] that Thayer provides nourishment for the "preferred freedoms" doctrine;[9] and that Thayer inconsistently applied his own rule.[10] Confusion also reigns over the extent to which Thayer's rule applies to state, as opposed to national, legislation.[11] Even the enormous respect Thayer paid both leading antagonists, Marshall and Gibson, has been a source of dismay. Analysis will reveal, however, that Thayer's rule of administration is a logical, workable, and probably necessary limitation on judicial judgment— if judicial review is to be compatible with its Hamiltonian rationale.

For Thayer, the reasonable doubt test emerged from the following considerations: Judicial review, while potentially and legitimately the final judgment of the constitutionality of legislation, was neither the first nor necessarily the last determination of constitutionality; the political branches always had an original constitutional duty to make a preliminary and possibly final judgment of the constitutionality of their own behavior. The Philadelphia convention, by rejecting a council of revision, had precluded the Judiciary from immediate review of legislation. By requiring all members of the political branches to support the Constitution, the oath provision of Article 6 imposed on them an obligation to make a preliminary determination of constitutionality. This preliminary judgment might be final because judicial review might not be invoked, and even if it were exercised, judicial review could not always erase or legitimate the prior impact of legislation. Therefore, Thayer reasoned, legislative judgment was *constitutionally* entitled to judicial respect. To veto a reasonable legislative enactment, handed down by presumably rational men constitutionally entitled to what Thayer called an independent judgment, on the basis of any judicial standard other than the reasonable doubt test, would not only have serious practical consequences regarding the fate of legislation; it would also amount to the substitution of one independent judgment for another. Thayer therefore concluded that the reasonable doubt test, a standard commonly used and accepted in many other American legal proceedings, implied a "partial," "not full and complete," power of review.

Not surprisingly, Thayer, like most commentators, overlooked the impartiality argument for judicial review. He agreed with Gibson that Marshall's justification in *Marbury* was wholly inadequate[12] and assumed that Marshall had simply followed Hamilton. "The reasoning," Thayer observed in his biographical sketch of Marshall in 1901, "is mainly that of Hamilton, in his short essay of a few years before in the 'Federalist.'" Marshall's logic, moreover, begged the question. "So far as any necessary conclusion is concerned," Thayer asserted, "the real question . . . is not whether the act is constitutional, but whether its constitutionality can properly be brought in question before a given tribunal."[13] Unfortunately, Marshall's opinion "went forward as smoothly as if the constitution were a private letter of attorney, and the court's duty under it were precisely like any of its most ordinary operations."[14]

Despite Thayer's failure to distinguish between Marshall's and Hamilton's positions and thus to acknowledge the latter's more persuasive rationale, Thayer *did* accept judicial review,[15] without offering a justification, and attempted to delineate its legitimate scope. Constitutional adjudication, in his view, did not consist merely of

construing two writings and comparing one with another, as two contracts or two statutes are construed and compared when they are said to conflict; of declaring *the true meaning* of each, and, if they are opposed to each other, of carrying into effect the constitution as being of superior obligation—an ordinary and humble judicial duty, as the courts sometimes describe it.

This approach to the judicial task easily produced

the wrong kind of disregard of legislative considerations; not merely in refusing to let them directly operate as grounds of judgment, but in refusing to consider them at all. Instead of taking them into account and allowing for them as furnishing possible grounds of legislative action, there takes place a pedantic and academic treatment of the texts of the constitution and the laws. And so we miss that combination of a lawyer's rigor and a statesman's breadth of view which should be found in dealing with this class of questions in constitutional law.[16]

Denouncing such "narrow and literal" methods of construction, Thayer echoed Marshall: "it is a constitution we are expounding." Because a constitution is a significantly different kind of document than a private contract or will, constitutional interpretation was not an ordinary judicial duty; for a constitution need not—in fact, often does not—have a "true meaning." "If it be said," Thayer hypothesized, that the construction of a constitution is ultimately "the construction of a writing; that this sort of question is always a court's question, and that it cannot well be admitted that there should be two legal constructions of the same instrument; that there is a right way and a wrong way of construing it, and only one right way; and that it is ultimately for the court to say what the right way is—this suggestion appears, at first sight, to have much force. But it really begs the question." For in reviewing legislative action, "a court cannot always . . . say that there is but one right and permissible way of construing the constitution." When, as in the construction of a contract or will, "a court is interpreting a writing merely to ascertain or apply its true meaning, then, indeed," Thayer admitted, "there is but one meaning allowable; namely, what the court adjudges to be its true meaning. But when the ultimate question is not that, but whether certain acts of another department, officer, or individual are legal or permissible, then this is not true." Rather, he insisted, *the ultimate question is not what is the true meaning of the constitution, but whether legislation is sustainable or not.*[17]

If, instead, constitutional interpretation were an ordinary judicial duty, requiring judges "merely and nakedly to ascertain the meaning of the text of the constitution and of the impeached Act of the legislature, and to determine, as an academic question, whether in the court's judgment the two were in conflict," then judicial review, Thayer admitted, would be "an elevated and important office, one dealing with great matters, involving large public considerations, but yet a function *far simpler* than it really is." For judicial opinion of the Constitution's true meaning was not necessarily controlling. Having construed the Constitution and the challenged statute, there remained "the truly momentous question—whether, after all, the court can disregard the Act":

It cannot do this as a mere matter of course,—merely because it is concluded that upon a just and true construction the law is unconstitutional. That is precisely the significance of the *rule of administration* that the courts lay down. It can only disregard the Act when those who have the right to make laws have not merely made a mistake, but have made a very clear one,—so clear that it is not open to rational question. That is the standard of duty to which the courts bring legislative Acts; that is the test which they apply,—*not merely their own judgment as to constitutionality, but their conclusion as to what judgment is permissible to another depart-*

ment which the constitution has charged with the duty of making it. This rule recognizes that, having regard to the great, complex, ever-unfolding exigencies of government, much which will seem unconstitutional to one man, or body of men, may reasonably not seem so to another; that the constitution often admits of different interpretations; that there is often a range of choice and judgment; that *in such cases* the constitution does not impose upon the legislature any one specific opinion, but leaves open this range of choice; and that *whatever choice is rational is constitutional.*[18]

Too often, Thayer lamented, judges strayed from the proper standard; too often they asked the wrong question. As early as 1884, Thayer had formulated the "precise question" a court faces regarding the constitutionality of legislation:

Has the legislative department kept within a reasonable interpretation of its power? Can their action reasonably be thought constitutional? Does the question of its conformity to the Constitution fairly admit of two opinions? If it does admit of two opinions, then the legislature is not to be deprived of its choice between them; for this choice is a part of that mass of legislative functions which belong to it and not to the court.

Instead of posing the question in these terms, judges usually asked: Is the law constitutional? This—"the common form in which courts put the question to themselves"—was a "dangerous" framework, for "it steadily tempts the court into stating its own opinion on questions that may be purely legislative or political, instead of fixing its attention upon the precise judicial function, that, namely, of determining whether the Legislature has transgressed the limits of reasonable interpretation."[19]

But even Thayer's rule of administration permitted limited judicial involvement in political matters. After all, the reasonable doubt test itself required judgment, which could be erroneous, and given the "subject-matter" with which it dealt, judicial review meant "taking a part, a second-ary part, in the political conduct of government." Thayer thus firmly broke with Gibson, who had denied, as Thayer put it, "the whole power to declare laws unconstitutional."[20] If judicial review existed at all, Gibson had argued in *Eakin v. Raub,* the constitutionality of challenged legisla-tion "would depend, not on the greatness of the supposed discrepancy with the constitution, but on the existence of any discrepancy at all." A judge, therefore, "would evade the question instead of deciding it, were he to refuse to decide in accordance with the inclination of his mind." For Gibson there was no middle ground between the extremes of legislative supremacy and judicial supremacy, no appropriate rule of administration for confining judicial judgment; either a judge gave the Constitution his independent interpretation of its true meaning, even in unclear cases, or he exercised no power of review at all. Thayer disagreed; whereas Gibson had insisted that judicial review was a dangerous and unnecessary check on legislative power, Thayer insisted that the "ultimate arbiter" of constitutionality will always be the courts. Their "interference," however, was "but one of many safeguards, and its scope was narrow." For what "really took place in adopting our theory of constitutional law," Thayer explained, was that "we introduced for the first time into the conduct of government through its great departments a judicial sanction—*not full and complete, but partial.* The judges were allowed, *indirectly and in a degree,* the power to revise the action of other departments and to pronounce it null." The power was indirect because it operated only, if ever, after passage of legislation; it was incomplete because the rule of administration circumscribed its scope. Nevertheless, Thayer warned, these limitations on judicial review left to our courts "a great and stately jurisdiction. It will only imperil the whole of it if it is sought to give them more. They must not step into the shoes of the law-maker."[21]

Had a broader reviewing power been intended, Thayer argued, the Judiciary "would have been let in . . . to a revision of the laws before they began to operate." Failure of the Philadelphia convention to associate the Court with a council of revision "may help us to understand," he explained, "why the extent of their control, when they do have the opportunity, should also be narrow." The absence of an immediate judicial opinion reinforced the legislature's duty, imposed by the oath provision of Article 6, to make an original and possibly final judgment. The legislature's "preliminary determination" was "a fact of very great importance"; indeed, the legislature "cannot act without making it." Moreover, Thayer emphasized, the initial determination of constitutionality might be "the final one," for it was "only as litigation may spring up, and as the course of it may happen to raise the point of constitutionality, that any question for the courts can regularly emerge." By then the legislative decision might have accomplished "results throughout the country of the profoundest importance," as, Thayer noted, in the case of the United States Bank, first chartered in 1791 but not judicially endorsed as constitutional until twenty-eight years later in *McCulloch v. Maryland.* "It is plain," Thayer concluded, that a power "so momentous" as the legislature's "primary authority to interpret" entitles "the actual determinations" of the legislature to "a corresponding respect; and this not on mere grounds of courtesy or conventional respect; but on very solid and significant grounds of policy and law."[22]

Thayer had effectively reinstated the relevance of the oath provision. Unlike Marshall, who had unsuccessfully used it to justify judicial review, and unlike Gibson, who had successfully used the same provision to undermine Marshall's argument, Thayer employed the oath provision neither to justify nor to challenge judicial review, but instead to aid in defining its legitimate scope. His rule of administration, signifying the judicial respect constitutionally due legislative judgment, was not a new principle in American jurisprudence; rather it was "a distinction and a test" which had come into "more and more prominence" as our jurisprudence grew "more intricate and refined." Constantly "resorted to in the criminal law in questions of self-defence, and in the civil law of tort in questions of negligence," the reasonable doubt test was also regularly applied by juries in criminal cases as well as by judges in reviewing the verdicts of juries in civil cases.[23] In a civil jury trial, Thayer explained in his treatise on evidence, "one of the most searching and far-reaching occasions for judicial control" was "keeping the jury within the bounds of reason." "This, of course, is a different thing," he emphasized, "from imposing upon the jury the judge's own private standard of what is reasonable":

For example, when the original question for the jury is one of reasonable conduct, and a court is called upon to revise the verdict, the judges do not undertake to set aside the verdict because their own opinion of the conduct in question differs from the jury's. They are not an appellate jury. The question for the court is not whether the conduct ultimately in question, e.g., that of a party injured in a railway accident, was reasonable, but whether the jury's conduct is reasonable in holding it to be so; and the test is whether a reasonable person could, upon the evidence, entertain the jury's opinion. Can the conduct which the jury are judging reasonably be thought reasonable? Is that a permissible view?[24]

The same rule applied to judicial review of legislation, Thayer thought, for the same reasons that justified the reasonable doubt test for juries in criminal cases and for judges in revising the civil verdicts of juries:

The ground on which courts lay down this test of a reasonable doubt for juries in criminal cases, is the great gravity of affecting a man with crime. The reason that they lay it down for themselves in reviewing the civil verdict of a jury is a different one, namely, because they are revising the work of another department charged with a duty of its own—having themselves no right to undertake *that* duty, no right at all in the matter except to hold the other department within the limit of a reasonable interpretation and exercise of its powers. The court must not, even negatively, undertake to pass upon the facts in jury cases. The reason that the same rule is laid down in regard to revising legislative acts is neither the one of these nor the other alone, but it is both. The courts are revising the work of a co-ordinate department, and must not, even negatively, undertake to legislate. And, again, they must not act unless the case is so very clear, because the consequences of setting aside legislation may be so serious.[25]

Just as the rationale for Thayer's rule of administration was not un-known to the American legal system, so its correct application rested on the commonly accepted distinction between two rules of evidence: a judgment based on "what is very plain and clear, clear beyond a reasonable doubt" and "a perfectly independent judgment" based on "the mere and simple preponderance of reasons for or against."[26] The "clear but deli-cate line"[27] between these judgments distinguished a court from a legis-lature in the same way that it separated a judge from a jury. The "far simpler" function was, of course, reaching an independent judgment; applying the reasonable doubt test usually took the judge a crucial step beyond an independent judgment. If, for example, a judge decided that the preponderance of reasons lay in favor of an act's constitutionality, no more judgment would be necessary and he would have to uphold the act. The act could not be found unconstitutional beyond a reasonable doubt because the preponderance of reasons provided more than a reason-able doubt in favor of the act. An independent judgment in favor of an act's constitutionality was, therefore, tantamount to applying the reason-able doubt test and finding more than the required reasonable doubt. If, however, the preponderance of reasons lay against the act's con-stitutionality, the judge could not void the act yet. He would have to ask further whether the act was unconstitutional beyond a reasonable doubt, a judgment requiring more than the preponderance of reasons against constitutionality.

Illustrating the relationship between independent judicial judgment and the reasonable doubt test, Thayer remarked that in *McCulloch v. Maryland* Marshall sought "to establish the court's *own opinion* of the constitutionality of the legislation establishing the United States Bank." Not only had Marshall deferred to a reasonable congressional interpretation of the ambiguous term "necessary"; he had also imported the Court's independent judgment of the issue into the decision. Thayer recognized that it "is very often true" that "where the court is sustaining an Act, and finds it to be constitutional *in its own opinion,* it is fit that this should be said." For "such a declaration"—an independent judgment in favor of constitutionality, thereby precluding a finding of unconstitutional beyond a reasonable doubt—"is all that the case calls for; it disposes of the matter." "But it is not always true," Thayer continued. There were "many cases where the judges sustain an Act *because they are in doubt about it;* where they are *not* giving their own opinion that it is constitutional, but are merely leaving untouched a determination of the legislature." In such cases judges did not "import their own opinion of the true construction of the constitution" into their decision; instead, "the strict meaning of their words, when they hold an Act constitutional, is merely this,—not unconstitutional beyond a reasonable doubt."[28]

An independent judicial judgment in favor of constitutionality was, therefore, *sufficient* but not *necessary* to sustain legislation; for an act stood, even if at variance with the judge's independent judgment, unless it also failed the reasonable doubt test. It followed, then, that an individual legislative judgment against constitutionality would not necessarily compel the same judgment by the same individual in a *judicial* capacity. This seeming paradox, central to a correct understanding of Thayer's rule of administration, had been endorsed by Judge Thomas M. Cooley, whom Thayer approvingly paraphrased:

[O]ne who is a member of a legislature may vote against a measure as being, in his judgment, unconstitutional; and, being subsequently placed on the bench, when this measure, having been passed by the legislature in spite of his opposition, comes before him judicially, may there find it his duty, although he has in no degree changed his opinion, to declare it constitutional.[29]

Although the legislator, exercising an independent judgment, had deemed the act unconstitutional, as a judge he could not allow that opinion to be controlling; for if a reasonable doubt in favor of constitutionality existed, the act must be sustained. Thayer therefore understandably conceded that much legislation "which is harmful *and unconstitutional* may take effect without any capacity in the courts to prevent it, since their whole power is a judicial one."[30] This result was possible for the same reason our system of criminal justice permitted a defendant, *in fact* guilty, to be acquitted: his guilt might not be established beyond a reasonable doubt. Justice Charlton, whom Thayer invoked as authority, had put it succinctly in a Georgia case decided in 1808: "When it remains doubtful whether the legislature have or have not trespassed on the constitution," courts were bound to defer to the legislature "because there is a possibility in such a case of the constitution being with the legislature."[31]

The rule of administration, while often affirmed by distinguished jurists, had also been "powerfully attacked," Thayer acknowledged. As early as 1817, Jeremiah Mason, considered by Thayer "one of the leaders" of the New England bar, had denied the propriety of the rule of administration in his argument of the *Dartmouth College* case before the Supreme Court of New Hampshire. The rule, he insisted, really required the court to surrender its jurisdiction because a reasonable doubt could ordinarily be made out in favor of most legislation. Accordingly, courts ought to review legislation with no more than "ordinary deliberation," with the "unbiased dictate" of their understanding—in effect, with an independent judgment instead of the "erroneous" reasonable doubt test. Daniel Webster, Thayer noted, had also "denied the existence or propriety" of the rule. In 1829, arguing the *Charles River Bridge* case before the Massachusetts courts, Webster urged that all cases involve some doubt and suggested that the passage of any act by the majority of a legislature would normally create a reasonable doubt in its favor. Because, however, legislators often were irresponsible, indeed, often depended on the courts to resolve difficult constitutional disputes, judges had a duty to exercise an independent judgment.[32]

Thayer demurred to these "ingenious" attempts to turn courts into councils "for answering legislative conundrums." Legislatures, to be sure, were "often faithless to their trust," but "virtue, sense, and competent knowledge are always to be attributed to that body." Just as when reviewing a jury's verdict, so when reviewing legislation, a court "will always assume a duly instructed body." The question, Thayer explained,

is not merely what persons may rationally do who are such as we often see, in point of fact, in our legislative bodies, persons untaught it may be, indocile, thoughtless, reckless, incompetent,—but what those other persons, competent, well-instructed, sagacious, attentive, intent only on public ends, fit to represent a self-governing people, such as our theory of government assumes to be carrying on our public affairs,—what such persons may reasonably think or do, what is the permissible view for them.[33]

If it be true, Thayer added, that "the holders of legislative power are care-less or evil, yet the constitutional duty of the court remains untouched; it cannot rightly attempt to protect the people, by undertaking a function not its own."[34]

Thayer's rule of administration, while limiting the scope of judicial judgment, did not imply the abdication of judicial review. Judgment still had to be exercised, and the judicial determination of whether a reasonable doubt existed was, therefore, not automatically made by the mere passage of legislation by presumably rational men; for rational men could—and sometimes did—act irrationally.[35] The question was not whether legislators were, in fact, rational, but whether their judgment in a particular case *could* have been based on a rational and thus permissible interpretation of the Constitution. This judicial judgment, moreover, turned not only on what legislators in fact believed when they passed a particular act but also on what they might rationally have believed as shown during the course of litigation by the quality of arguments for and against the constitutionality of the act.[36]

Nor was the distinction between the reasonable doubt test and independent judicial judgment meaningless in application. It was instead, Thayer emphasized, "a familiar and important discrimination, of daily application in our courts." Criminal defendants were daily acquitted or convicted by juries on the basis of the reasonable doubt test, and judges sometimes directed or revised jury verdicts in criminal cases on the ground that no jury, applying the reasonable doubt test, could fairly find the defendant guilty. Likewise, civil juries, exercising an independent judgment, daily reached verdicts on the basis of the preponderance of the evidence, and trial judges sometimes directed or revised their verdicts on the ground that the evidence on one side prevailed beyond a reasonable doubt. In "competent hands," then, the distinction made a difference; it was not "evanescent," as critics had suggested. Responding to this charge, Lord Esher, an English judge whom Thayer cited, insisted that "the mode in which the subject is approached makes the greatest difference. To ask 'should we have found the same verdict,' is surely not the same thing as to ask whether there is room for a reasonable difference of opinion."[37]

That reasonable differences of opinion existed over the correct construction of the Constitution often meant that many constitutional issues properly became "jury questions"—issues on which reasonable men, exercising an independent judgment, could justifiably decide either way. Application of Thayer's rule of administration meant that in such cases a judge had no more power to substitute his independent judgment for that of the legislature than he had to revise a jury verdict when the issue was also a jury question. Thayer's definition of the legitimate scope of judicial judgment therefore enabled the views of Locke, Yates, and Gibson to prevail in some measure. This was true *not* because, as Locke, Yates, and Gibson had argued, the political branches and ultimately the people were the exclusive judge of the constitutionality of legislation, but rather because the invalidity of legislative judgment could not always be established beyond a reasonable doubt, even by impartial judges. The rationale behind this limitation on judicial review, sometimes permitting, as Thayer recognized, unconstitutional legislation to go unchecked by the courts, was essentially the same as that permitting the acquittal of ten guilty men so that one innocent man would not be convicted: it would be just as dangerous for impartial but fallible judges to give the Constitution a true meaning when it had no clear one as for an impartial but fallible jury to convict a criminal defendant when a reasonable doubt still existed; even the utmost impartiality could not create sufficient certainty to dispel a reasonable doubt.

It followed, then, that the impartiality of judges did not justify judicial, instead of political, choice between constitutionally permissible alternative policies. Indeed, the impartiality argument went only so far; it justified not judicial policy-making but only the final construction of the Constitution by independent judges for the purpose of keeping political judgment within constitutional bounds. Because the exercise of choice between constitutionally permissible alternatives was exclusively a political function, judicial review required application of the reasonable doubt test, not just as a necessary aid in performing the judicial function impartially, but also as a necessary aid in reducing the possibility of judicial policy-making.

The *justification* of judicial review, therefore, delimited its legitimate *scope*, and the justification of a *broader* scope—for example, the exercise of independent judicial judgment—required a different rationale, one justifying not judicial review but judicial performance of a political function. Impartiality alone as a justification for judicial policy-making was insufficient; two further conditions, both categorically rejected by the Framers, were needed: first, the belief that impartiality was a necessary aid in fashioning "good" or "wise" public policy and hence the belief that impartial judges were capable of making better public policy than were legislators; and, second, the preference for "wise" public policy made

by politically independent judges over the public policy made by legislators. Impartiality justified judicial review, subject to Thayer's rule of
administration, of the outcome of the political process, but removal
from the political process, a prerequisite for impartiality, did not
justify substitution of politically independent judicial judgment for the
constitutional outcome of the political process itself.

Accordingly, Thayer gave no support to the preferred freedoms
doctrine,[38] for his rule precluded the substitution of independent judicial
judgment for rational, and, therefore, possibly "unwise," legislative choice
or accommodation between conflicting constitutional values when neither
value was clearly constitutionally preferred.[39] But the charge that Thayer's
rule does not solve the problem of conflicting constitutional values is
simply not true; rather the rule does not solve the problem as some of
Thayer's critics would prefer that it be solved. If, for example, a constitutional power allegedly conflicted with a constitutional right or
restraint on that power, or if two constitutionally protected rights
allegedly conflicted, application of Thayer's rule would require a judicial
determination of whether one constitutional value clearly prevailed over
the other. If, by virtue of the reasonable doubt test, a power clearly prevailed over a right, or a right over a power, or one right over another,
then that would resolve the issue. Otherwise, reasonable legislative
judgment would be sustained, and that would resolve the issue, too; for
"nothing but the plainest constitutional provisions of restraint," Thayer
insisted, would justify judicial disregard of reasonable legislative judgment.[40]

To the extent, of course, that the reasonable doubt test yielded a clear
constitutional preference for, say, non property rights over property rights,
or, for example, rights involving access to the political process, such
as First Amendment freedoms, over other freedoms protected by the Bill
of Rights, or, say, the rights of minorities over those of majorities—
positions often associated with the preferred freedoms doctrine—then
judicial review, even limited by Thayer's rule, would enhance the status
of *constitutionally preferred* freedoms. But Thayer never endorsed the
exercise of independent judicial judgment, intentionally aimed at en-
larging particular constitutional rights, at the expense of rational
legislative judgment. Instead, he had enormous respect for the political
process and strongly believed that judicial policy-making, in whatever
cause, seriously threatened the effective functioning of that process.[41]
While courts surely had a duty to protect the constitutional integrity of

the political process, "no political theories" based merely on an independent judgment "as to the nature of our system of government" would justify judicial tampering with the system or with its constitutional outcome, even in the name of "wisdom" or "justice."[42]

Despite his strong and repeated warnings against judicial invalidation of legislation based only on a court's independent judgment, Thayer nevertheless insisted on an important exception to his rule of administration. Whereas courts were obliged to apply the reasonable doubt test when reviewing acts of coordinate branches of government, they might be charged with "a special duty" to exercise "a *perfectly independent judgment* in construing and applying the laws and constitutions of the States."[43] Thayer, like Gibson, believed that the Supremacy Clause required the federal courts to maintain the "paramount authority" of the national government "in its true and just proportions, to be determined by itself." "If a State legislature passes a law," he reasoned, "which is impeached in the due course of litigation before the national courts, as being in conflict with the supreme law of the land, those courts *may* have to ask themselves a question different from that which would be applicable if the enactments were those of a co-ordinate department." When, however, the issue "relates to what is admitted *not* to belong to the national power," then Thayer urged a different approach:

Whoever construes a State constitution, whether the State or national judiciary, must allow to that legislature the full range of rational construction. But when the question is whether State action be or be not conformable to the paramount constitution, the supreme law of the land, we have a different matter in hand. *Fundamentally, it involves the allotment of power between the two governments,*—where the line is to be drawn. True, the judiciary is still debating whether a legislature has transgressed its limit; but the departments are not co-ordinate, and the limit is at a different point. The judiciary now speaks as representing a paramount constitution and government, whose duty it is, in *all* its departments, to allow to that constitution nothing less than its just and true interpretation; and having fixed this, to guard it against any inroads from without.[44]

Whether Thayer intended federal courts to exercise independent judgment, instead of applying the reasonable doubt test, when reviewing *all* state legislation allegedly conflicting with the federal Constitution has been a continuing source of puzzlement. Indeed, some of his critics, believing that Thayer did intend the application of independent judicial judgment to all state legislation, have charged him with inconsistency for approving decisions in which federal courts in fact applied the reasonable doubt test to determine whether state legislation conflicted with the Constitution.[45] Thayer's own language, however, seems to limit the application of independent judicial judgment to state action allegedly in conflict with the constitutional exercise of national power. Intended to protect national power against state encroachment, the independent judgment standard was, it appears, not meant by Thayer to be applied to state legislation in the absence of a clash with national power.[46]

Thayer could therefore quite consistently approve Chief Justice Marshall's use of the reasonable doubt test in the *Dartmouth College* case (1819),[47] as well as Justice Bushrod Washington's reference to the same test in his dissenting opinion in *Ogden v. Saunders* (1827).[48] Both cases held unconstitutional state action that did not conflict with national power. Thayer's approval of the decision in the *Minnesota Rate* cases (1890) also becomes understandable. The constitutional issue there, as Thayer noted, was "whether a statute providing for a commission to regulate railroad charges, which excluded the parties from access to the courts for an ultimate judicial revision of the action of the commission," violated the Due Process Clause of the Fourteenth Amendment.[49] As in *Dartmouth College* and *Ogden,* no state conflict with national power existed. Accordingly, Thayer applied the reasonable doubt test, not an independent judgment, and concluded, like the Court, that the Minnesota statute was clearly unconstitutional:

[T]here is often that ultimate question, which was vindicated for the judges in a recent highly important case [the *Minnesota Rate* cases] in the Supreme Court of the United States, viz., that of the reasonableness of a legislature's exercise of its most undoubted powers; of the permissible limit of those powers. If a legislature undertakes to exert the taxing power, that of eminent domain, or any part of that vast, unclassified residue of legislative authority which is called, not always intelligently, the police power, this action must not degenerate into an excess, so as to become, in reality, something different and forbidden,—e.g., the depriving of people of their property without due process of law; and whether it does so or not, must be determined by the judges. But in such cases it is always to be remembered that the judicial question is a secondary one. The legislature in determining what shall be done, what it is reasonable to do, does not divide its duty with the judges, nor must it conform to their conception of what is prudent or reasonable legislation. The judicial function is merely that of fixing the outside border of reasonable legislative action, the boundary beyond which the taxing power, the power of eminent domain, police power, and legislative power in general, cannot go without violating the prohibitions of the constitution or crossing the line of its grants.[50]

Thayer's commentaries on the constitutional relationship between state power and Congress's commerce power provide further evidence that he confined the independent judgment standard to state action allegedly colliding with the exercise of national power. Thayer believed that Congress and not the Court was the primary regulator of this relationship. "It is Congress and not the courts, to whom is intrusted the regulation of that portion of commerce which is interstate, foreign, and with the Indian tribes;" and, therefore, he concluded, "primarily it would appear to be the office of the Federal legislature, and not of the Federal courts, to supervise and moderate the action of the local legislatures, where it touches these parts of commerce." Thus, Thayer approved the decision in the leading case of *Cooley v. Board of Port Wardens* (1851), in which the Court upheld a state pilotage fee against the charge that it unconstitutionally conflicted with the national commerce power. Speaking for the Court, Justice Benjamin Curtis reasoned that subjects national in scope, requiring uniform legislation, must be regulated by Congress, but that subjects local in character, not demanding uniform legislation, could be regulated by the states until Congress, by acting on the same subject, displaced state law. In *Cooley,* Congress had determined that the subject did not require uniform, national regulation and had manifested a clear intent to leave regulation of the subject to the states. No conflict existed, then, between state action and congressional exercise of the commerce power. Curtis's opinion, Thayer thought, correctly implied that Congress, not the Court, was the primary judge of the need for uniform, national legislation:

Now the question whether or not a given subject admits of only one uniform system or plan of regulation is primarily a legislative question, not a judicial one. For it involves a consideration of what, on practical grounds, is expedient, possible, or desirable; and whether, being so at one time or place, it is so at another. . . . It is not in the language of the [commerce] clause . . . , or in any necessary construction of it, that any requirement of uniformity is found, in any case whatever. That can only be declared necessary, in any given case, as being the determination of some one's practical judgment. The question, then, appears to be a legislative one; it is for Congress and not for the courts,—except, indeed, in the sense that the courts may control a legislative decision, so far as to keep it within the bounds of reason, of rational opinion.[51]

Thayer believed, then, that if Congress expressly determined, as in *Cooley*, that uniformity was not required and that state legislation should stand, courts could not review state legislation on the issue of uniformity. Indeed, courts were not free to review state legislation on that issue even if Congress had not acted at all. Thayer therefore disapproved the Court's decision in *Leisy v. Hardin* (1890), where Chief Justice Melville Fuller, speaking for the Court, struck down a state law prohibiting the sale in the original package of liquors introduced from another state. The Court held that the need for uniformity, in the absence of congressional action, barred state regulation of the subject. Thayer disagreed, contending that congressional silence should not be construed as an excuse for judicial policy-making. To the question, "who shall say whether one uniform rule is required," Thayer replied: "That question is for Congress, and the State regulation must stand until Congress shall see fit to alter it." To the suggestion "that Congress will very likely be dilatory or negligent, or that it may purposely allow, and connive at, what should be forbidden,—that," he conceded, "is quite possible." "But the objection," he added, "is a criticism upon the arrangements of the Constitution itself, in giving so much power to the legislature and so little to the courts."[52] Congressional silence, then, permitted the application of neither an independent judgment nor the reasonable doubt test to state legislation on the issue of uniformity. Instead, state legislation could only be invalidated, Thayer emphasized, if it were "so clearly unconstitutional" for reasons *other* than the need for uniformity "that no consent of Congress" could save it.[53]

The independent judgment test seems, therefore, not intended by Thayer to be applied to all state action. Even its apparent limitation, however, to state action allegedly in conflict with the constitutional exercise of national power is not justified; for Thayer's insistence on employing independent judicial judgment in the service of national supremacy, in order to vindicate national power at the expense of state power where genuine conflict is doubtful, really amounts to advocacy of a particular political theory in violation of his own warning.[54] After all, although the Supremacy Clause, without the aid of an independent judgment, clearly yields supremacy for constitutional national law over conflicting state law, this fact does not imply a broader scope for judicial judgment, entailing a special judicial duty to protect national power over state power where conflict does not clearly exist. Nor was the independent judgment test even needed to protect national power. Thayer himself had correctly perceived that Congress had primary responsibility for regulating state action touching on Congress's commerce power. Rejecting the need for independent judicial judgment in the service of that power, he observed that

the great thing which the makers of the Constitution had in view, as to this subject [commerce], was to secure power and control to a single hand, the general government, the common representative of all, instead of leaving it divided and scattered among the States; and that this object is clearly accomplished.

If, as Thayer rightly believed, Congress was perfectly able to regulate commerce and thereby control state interference with that subject, then Congress was also able to frame legislation so as clearly to preclude state encroachment on the exercise of national power. Application of Thayer's rule of administration, thus revised, to an alleged conflict between state and national power would recognize, therefore, that Congress, in exercising all of its constitutional powers, was the primary judge, subject to the reasonable doubt test, of whether conflict existed; and if, as Thayer pointed out, Congress were to be "dilatory or negligent," the fault lay with "the Constitution itself" for "giving so much power to the legislature and so little to the courts."[55]

Thayer's rule of administration still left the courts what Thayer called "a great and stately jurisdiction"; for, as Thayer himself admitted, judicial review, even circumscribed by the reasonable doubt test, allowed the courts a secondary role in the conduct of government. The rule meant not an abdication of judicial review because the judiciary remained the ultimate arbiter of rational and permissible constitutional construction; it meant rather a disavowal of both judicial supremacy and legislative supremacy. A practical, probably necessary restriction on an otherwise undefined scope for judicial judgment, the rule at once reconciled judicial review with its Hamiltonian justification and struck a logical balance between judicial supremacy, which permitted the substitution of independent judicial judgment for reasonable legislative judgment, and legislative supremacy, which freed the political branches from impartial judicial resolution of constitutional disputes.

Two centuries before Thayer set forth his views, John Locke, while advocating legislative supremacy, had provided a persuasive rationale for judicial review and had even suggested, if only indirectly, Thayer's rule of administration. The Englishman had posited not only majoritarian, popular sovereignty within the limits of natural law, but also the need for impartial judges to resolve disputes in clear cases, not where natural law was "silent or doubtful." Both premises found their way into early American constitutional thought. While the Framers may have approved judicial review but condemned judicial policy-making, they left the scope of judicial judgment inadequately defined. This omission prompted Robert Yates, who feared that judicial review would become judicial supremacy, especially given the ambiguous nature of the Constitution, to come out for the other extreme, legislative supremacy. Marshall's failure in *Marbury* to provide a persuasive rationale for judicial review led to Gibson's scathing rebuke and his advocacy of legislative supremacy. Only Hamilton developed a concept of judicial review that combined a convincing justification for the power with a plausible, potentially workable definition of its legitimate scope. Unlike Marshall in *Marbury*, Hamilton adopted Locke's impartiality argument, and like the Framers, especially Yates and later Gibson, Hamilton recognized that judges were not infallible interpreters of the Constitution. This required a limitation on judicial judgment, and therefore Hamilton insisted on an "irreconcilable variance," in effect, restricting the judicial veto to clear violations of the Constitution, a test Marshall espoused and correctly applied in *McCulloch*.

Thayer, then, did not write on a clean slate; the theoretical basis for a middle ground between legislative supremacy and judicial supremacy had been laid. Addressing himself to the legitimate scope of judicial review and, curiously, not to its justification, Thayer nevertheless rationalized standards for judicial judgment which in fact reconcile judicial review with its Hamiltonian justification. Moreover, his rule of administration, properly revised, provides standards not only for judges but also for judges of judges. General standards, of course, do not prescribe solutions in individual cases, and Thayer's rule, like all guideposts, is not self-applying. Even limited by the rule of administration, judges, like criminal juries, might differ over what constitutes a reasonable doubt; the possibilities, the stuff of which reasonable doubts are made, do not always strike all men, however reasonable, alike. Even under Thayer's rule of administration, then, the freedom and the burden of decision-making remain. But that freedom is narrowed, and that was Thayer's aim. He sought to reduce the scope of judicial freedom without diminishing the judicial duty and burden of judging.

3

ECONOMIC DUE PROCESS, THE COMMERCE CLAUSE, AND THE DEMISE OF THE REASONABLE DOUBT TEST

Thayer's rule of administration has been honored in the breach as much as it has been faithfully followed. In fact, barely two years after his 1893 article appeared, the Supreme Court, as if in direct defiance of Thayer's admonition to confine judicial judgment to the reasonable doubt test, embarked upon a reign of judicial supremacy that lasted until 1936. During this period the Court often invalidated the exercise of national power under the Commerce Clause, usually on the ground that Congress was attempting to regulate a subject reserved exclusively to the states. The Court also struck down the exercise of states' power, usually on the ground that it violated the Due Process Clause of the Fourteenth Amendment. The result of this exercise of independent judicial judgment in the service of property rights and "dual federalism"[1] was the temporary creation of a no-man's-land, a power vacuum effectively free from governmental regulation at both state and national levels.

The crucial decision sparking what some observers have called "a judicial revolution"[2] is thought to have been made in 1890 in the *Minnesota Rate* cases. "From that year," Judge Charles M. Hough has written, "I date the flood."[3] That case, Robert G. McCloskey has added, "was an important link in a long chain of decisions involving the due process clause in which 'the presumption of constitutionality' seemed often displaced by the judges' flat judgment of right or wrong."[4] Thayer, however, had approved the decision; to him the case preserved the reasonable doubt test.[5] I concur. Unlike Judge Hough, I date the flood—at least, regarding the exercise of independent judicial judgment of the Fourteenth

Amendment's Due Process Clause—not in 1890 but fifteen years later in *Lochner v. New York*. I agree with leading commentators, however, that *United States v. E. C. Knight*, decided in 1895, marked the advent of judicial supremacy over Congress's exercise of its commerce power.

The *Minnesota Rate* cases held simply that a state could not constitutionally deny railroads judicial review of rates fixed by legislatures. Justice Blatchford's majority opinion in no way implied that courts were free to substitute their independent judgment for a reasonable legislative determination. Justice Harlan, who joined the Court's opinion, had three years earlier explicitly invoked the reasonable doubt test in his opinion of the Court in *Mugler v. Kansas*.[6] Presumably, Harlan understood the *Minnesota Rate* cases to embody the same test. Justice Miller, concurring in the *Minnesota Rate* cases, certainly did. "Neither the legislature, nor such commission acting under authority of the legislature," he wrote, "can establish *arbitrarily* . . . a tariff of rates which is *so unreasonable* as to practically destroy the value of property of persons engaged in the carrying business, nor *so exorbitant and extravagant* as to be in *utter disregard* of the rights of the public for the use of such regulation."[7] Even Justice Bradley, dissenting, conceded that the Court could, in fact, invalidate legislative rate-fixing when the violation of property rights was "clear and unmistakable." "The Constitution," he noted, "contemplates the possibility of such an invasion of rights."[8] Perhaps Bradley and the other two dissenters for whom he wrote, Justices Gray and Lamar, had already reviewed the reasonableness of the rates and had concluded that they were clearly not unreasonable. If so, their position is not necessarily inconsistent with that of the majority who, upon review of the rates, might well have reached the same conclusion.

The *Minnesota Rate* cases, then, need not have led to the results reached in *Lochner*, "a decision," as McCloskey has rightly observed, "that has probably received more nearly unanimous criticism than any other in the twentieth century." Justice Peckham's majority opinion in *Lochner* surely deserves the obloquy heaped upon it. While claiming more than once to apply the reasonable doubt test, Peckham unmistakably exercised independent judgment, blatantly reversed the traditional presumption of constitutionality, explicitly queried and denounced legislative motive, and impugned the wisdom of the law—all for the sake of reading into the Fourteenth Amendment a value, liberty of contract, for which there was "little or no detectable constitutional warrant," as McCloskey has noted.[9]

At the outset of his opinion in *Lochner,* Peckham asked whether New York's law regulating bakers' working hours was a fair, reasonable, and appropriate exercise of the state's police power. Disdaining substituting the judgment of the court for that of the legislature, he promised: "If the act be within the power of the state it is valid, although the judgment of the court might be totally opposed to the enactment of such a law." Then he resolved the constitutional issue "in a few words." "There is no reasonable ground," Peckham flatly concluded, "for interfering with the liberty of a person or the right of free contract, by determining the hours of labor, in the occupation of a baker."

The transparency of Peckham's application of the reasonable doubt test is equally obvious in other parts of his opinion. Lower courts had consistently upheld the law as a reasonable health regulation. The New York Court of Appeals, while admitting that "the evidence was not uniform," concluded that the state legislature could reasonably infer that the occupation of a baker was sufficiently unhealthy to warrant restricting bakers' working hours. Yet Peckham insisted on exercising independent judgment: "There is, in our judgment, no reasonable foundation for holding this to be necessary or appropriate as a health law." Despite conceding that "statistics regarding all trades and occupations" indicated that "the trade of a baker does not appear to be as healthy as some other trades," Peckham asserted: "We think that there can be no fair doubt that the trade of a baker, in and of itself, is not an unhealthy one" to the degree that would authorize the regulation of working hours. After all, he reasoned, to uphold *this* law would permit regulating the working hours of many *other* trades, especially those which were even more unhealthy than that of the bakers.

With similar logic Peckham disposed of the contention that the state legislature could reasonably have believed that excessive working hours in a bakery might impair the healthful quality of the bread produced, thus endangering the public health. "In our judgment," he wrote, "it is not possible in fact to discover the connection between the number of hours a baker may work in the bakery and the healthful quality of the bread made by the workman." Not only did the burden of proof shift to the state, but the legislature now had to show a clear, not just a reasonable, connection between the subject regulated and the public welfare. Otherwise, Peckham held, the interference with freedom to contract would not be justified. The reasonable doubt test had been inverted.

At bottom, the Court's commitment to *laissez-faire* controlled its independent judgment. "We do not believe," Peckham candidly admitted, "in the soundness of the views which uphold this law." Peckham had "a suspicion that there was some other motive dominating the legislature" than the purpose to serve the public health. "It is impossible for us to shut our eyes," he wrote, "to the fact that many of the laws of this character" are passed not as health or welfare measures but "in reality" from "other motives." The "real object and purpose" in this case, he concluded, was "simply to regulate the hours of labor between the master and his employees." This, of course, the *laissez-faire* principle precluded.

Maybe so, the four dissenters in *Lochner* averred, but the Constitution surely did not. In a brief and famous dissent Justice Holmes railed against the Court's reliance on "a particular economic theory" to invalidate the New York law. "The Fourteenth Amendment," he insisted, "does not enact Mr. Herbert Spencer's *Social Statics.*" Applying the reasonable doubt test, Holmes concluded that a "reasonable man might think it a proper measure on the score of health."

In a longer and less famous dissent, Justice Harlan, who had joined the majority in the *Minnesota Rate* cases, spent most of his opinion emphasizing the reasonable doubt test. Noting that liberty of contract was not absolute, that it was subject to reasonable regulations which the Court had previously sustained, he then posed the central question: "What are the conditions under which the judiciary may declare such regulations to be in excess of legislative authority and void?" Harlan's answer immediately followed:

Upon this point there is no room for dispute; for the rule is universal that a legislative enactment, Federal or state, is never to be disregarded or held invalid unless it be, beyond question, plainly and palpably in excess of legislative power. If there be doubt as to the validity of the statute, that doubt must therefore be resolved in favor of its validity, and the courts must keep their hands off, leaving the legislature to meet the responsibility for unwise legislation.

Applying the rule, Harlan thought it plain that the New York statute was a health measure. It was impossible to deny the relationship between the regulation of working hours and bakers' health. Nor could Harlan say "that the statute is, beyond question, a plain, palpable invasion of rights secured by the fundamental law." The unhealthiness of the trade of a baker was amply supported, Harlan believed, and he devoted two full pages of his opinion to the evidence. Furthermore, the number of working hours set by the state legislature was "reasonable." "It is enough for the determination of this case ... ," he urged, "that the question is one about which there is room for debate and for honest difference of opinion." Concluding his dissent, Harlan again stressed the reasonable doubt test. The act should stand for "an all-sufficient reason": it was not "plainly and palpably" unconstitutional.

The act, however, fell, and by 1905 the Court had established a leading precedent for voiding state, even national, legislation for violating liberty of contract. Meanwhile, the Court, ten years earlier, had set an equally important precedent for impairing the exercise of Congress's commerce power. In an opinion that probably deserves as much criticism as Peckham's in *Lochner,* Chief Justice Fuller, writing for the Court in *United States v. E. C. Knight,* rejected the reasonable doubt test in favor of an arbitrary definition of commerce thoroughly at odds with Chief Justice Marshall's authoritative holding in *Gibbons v. Ogden.* Fuller, of course, claimed to rely on Marshall, but the latter's sweeping interpretation of the Commerce Clause bears no resemblance to Fuller's construction. In *Gibbons,* Marshall had declared that the Commerce Clause comprehended

that commerce which concerns more states than one. ... The genius and character of the whole government seem to be, that its action is to be applied to all the external concerns of the nation, and to those internal concerns which affect the states generally; but not to those which are completely within a particular state, which do not affect other states, and with which it is not necessary to interfere, for the purpose of executing some of the general powers of the government.[10]

Yet Fuller blithely ignored the implications of Marshall's definition and ruled that the Sherman Anti-Trust Act of 1890 could not constitutionally be applied to a sugar trust that controlled 98 percent of all the sugar refining business in the nation. The manufacture of sugar, Fuller held, was not commerce; it had only an "indirect" effect on commerce among the states. Therefore, he reasoned, the manufacture of sugar was a subject reserved "exclusively" to the states.

Marshall, of course, had not distinguished between "direct" and "indirect" effects of local matters on commerce among the states, but Fuller insisted on that artificial distinction. "Contracts, combinations, or conspiracies to control domestic enterprise in manufacture ... or to raise or lower prices or wages," he conceded, "might unquestionably tend to restrain external as well as domestic trade"—precisely what the Sherman Act prohibited—"but the restraint would be an indirect result, however inevitable, and whatever its extent." Fuller recognized that products are manufactured only to be sold and that manufacture and commerce are inextricably linked, yet he concluded that "it does not follow that an attempt to monopolize, or the actual monopoly of, the manufacture was an attempt ... to monopolize commerce, even though, in order to dispose of the product, the instrumentality of commerce was necessarily invoked." Because commerce "succeeds to manufacture, and is not a part of it," Fuller's corollary conclusion rendered manufacture a subject reserved "exclusively" to the states, "as required by our dual form of government."

Justice Harlan, the lone dissenter in the *Knight* case, had little difficulty in exposing the circularity of Fuller's reasoning. Harlan invoked Marshall's opinion in *Gibbons* and accused the majority of placing a false constitutional barrier before Congress. The commerce power, he noted, echoing Marshall, is plenary. "Who can say," he queried, that the object of the Sherman Act, the protection of commerce among the states against unlawful restraints, "is not legitimate, or is not within the scope of the Constitution?" "Who can say," he continued, that the means employed, the suppression, by legal proceedings, of combinations, conspiracies, and monopolies which, by their inevitable and admitted tendency, improperly restrain commerce among the states, "are not appropriate to attain the end of freeing commercial intercourse among the states from [such] burdens and exactions?" No clause of the Constitution, Harlan insisted, could be invoked to invalidate the means prescribed by Congress. The majority had appealed to what the dissenter called "the doctrine of the autonomy of the states," later dubbed "dual federalism." This doctrine, Harlan urged, could not properly be invoked to override an expressly granted power. Nor could the Court rightly allege that the manufacture of sugar only indirectly affected commerce among the states. The defendant corporation, Harlan noted, not only controlled nearly all the sugar refining business in the country; it also controlled the price of that commodity in all the states and therefore achieved a direct restraint of trade in all the states. By denying Congress the power to regulate the sugar trust, Harlan concluded, the Court had effectively freed the industry from all regulation, for no single state was able, constitutionally or practically, to regulate a nationwide business.

As a result, then, of the *Lochner* and *Knight* decisions, both reached over the vigorous dissents of Justice Harlan, a potential no-man's-land had been created. *Knight* would be a vital precedent for impairing the national commerce power, while *Lochner* would serve to impose due process restrictions on the states as well as on the national government. Yet conflicting precedents soon followed *Knight* and *Lochner,* so that on its way to consideration of New Deal legislation in the mid-1930s the Court developed two lines of precedent within the areas of commerce and due process.

The first major break with the *Knight* decision came in 1903 in *Champion v. Ames.* A replay of *Knight* with its results reversed, the *Lottery* case saw Harlan's application of the reasonable doubt test prevail over Fuller's independent judgment. Harlan, now in a bare majority, echoed his *Knight* dissent. Congressional prohibition of interstate shipment of lottery tickets was upheld because the power to regulate commerce among the states included the power to prohibit it. Ignoring the *Knight* precedent, Harlan leaned heavily upon Marshall's opinion in *Gibbons,* which Harlan considered the "leading case." The Tenth Amendment was irrelevant, he insisted, because the commerce power had been expressly delegated to Congress. Harlan concluded by invoking the reasonable doubt test. An act of Congress would fall only if that branch of government had "manifestly" exceeded its powers.

Fuller, now dissenting, also repeated his *Knight* opinion. Relying strongly on *Knight* as controlling precedent, he again appealed to the doctrine of dual federalism to convert the states' reserved powers into exclusive powers. As Congress's power to regulate commerce did not here include the power to prohibit it, the power to suppress lottery tickets, even their movement across state lines, was reserved "exclusively" to the states. Otherwise, reasoned Fuller, the Tenth Amendment would be upended.

If the decision in *Champion* attenuated, without overruling, the *Knight* decision, other cases, quickly following *Champion,* reinforced that departure from *Knight.* Following a successful application of the Sherman Act in *Northern Securities Co. v. United States*[11] in 1904, the Court the next year seemed to lay the *Knight* doctrine to rest, again without overruling it. Speaking for a unanimous Court in *Swift v. United States,* Justice Holmes used strong language:

[C]ommerce among the states is not a technical legal conception, but a practical one, drawn from the course of business. When cattle are sent for sale from a place in one state, with the expectation that they will end their transit, after purchase, in another, and when in effect they do so, with only the interruption necessary to find a purchaser at the stockyards, and when this is a typical, constantly recurring course, the current thus existing is a current of commerce among the states, and the purchase of the cattle is a part and incident of such commerce.

The sales agreements in *Swift* were no less local than the manufacturing agreements in *Knight*, but the Court in *Swift* treated them as integral parts of an interstate "stream of commerce."

Thirteen years later, however, the restrictive *Knight* doctrine reappeared when the Court in *Hammer v. Dagenhart* (1918) struck down an act of Congress barring the shipment in interstate commerce of certain products of child labor. Writing for a five-man majority, Justice Day attempted, unsuccessfully, to distinguish the *Lottery* case from the *Child Labor* case, yet really relied on, without acknowledging, both Fuller's dissent in the *Lottery* case and Fuller's majority opinion in the *Knight* case. The result was an opinion which should rank for disrepute with Fuller's in *Knight* and Peckham's in *Lochner*.

The regulation of commerce among the states, Day insisted, recalling Fuller in the *Lottery* case, did not necessarily permit prohibition of goods in interstate commerce. Congress could forbid the movement of goods in interstate commerce only to prevent the accomplishment of harmful results. "This element," while present in the *Lottery* case, Day thought, "is wanting in the present case." "The goods shipped," he concluded, "are of themselves harmless," whereas lottery tickets were presumably of themselves harmful. Harking back to Fuller in *Knight,* again without citing the case, Day also revived the ill-founded distinction between manufacture and commerce. The former was not the latter, even when the goods were clearly intended for interstate shipment, and *therefore* the power to regulate manufacture was reserved exclusively to the states. To reason differently, Day reasoned, would violate the Tenth Amendment which literally reserved to the states "the powers not expressly [sic] delegated to the national government."[12]

Justice Holmes, dissenting in *Hammer* with Justices McKenna, Brandeis, and Clarke, graciously avoided correcting Day's amendment of the Tenth Amendment. Instead, Holmes pointed out that the power to regulate commerce was, in fact, expressly delegated. "The first step in my argument," he began, "is to make plain what no one is likely to dispute—that the statute in question is within the power expressly given to Congress." Furthermore, the commerce power was granted in "unqualified terms." It followed that the power to regulate commerce necessarily included the power to prohibit it. By definition, Holmes insisted, any regulation means "the prohibition of something." Relying on the *Lottery* case as controlling precedent, the dissenter called the child labor law "clearly" constitutional.

Holmes's reply to the majority's reliance on "dual federalism" was equally succinct. There was "no room for doubt" about the act's constitutionality despite its impact on state power. Again invoking the *Lottery* case, he urged that Congress may carry out its views of public policy "whatever indirect effect they may have upon the activities of the states." The Supremacy Clause so dictated. The *Knight* doctrine, Holmes pointed out, had been discredited by successful application of the Sherman Act in other cases. At bottom, the Court in *Hammer*, as in *Knight*, had substituted its own independent judgment for that of Congress. "I should have thought," Holmes ruefully concluded, "that if we were to introduce our own moral conceptions where in my opinion they do not belong, this was pre-eminently a case for upholding" legislation designed to prohibit in interstate commerce fruits of "the evil of premature and excessive child labor."

Revived in *Hammer* after its rejection in *Swift*, the *Knight* doctrine once more seemed to fall into desuetude when in 1922 the Court in *Stafford v. Wallace* upheld application of the Packers and Stockyards Act of 1921 to certain practices of meat-packers that restricted and burdened interstate commerce in meat products. Writing for a nearly unanimous Court, only Justice McReynolds dissenting, Chief Justice Taft ignored *Knight* and depended instead on Justice Holmes's "stream of commerce" concept developed in *Swift*. The stockyards, Taft noted, were "not a place of rest or final destination"; they were "but a throat through which the current flows." Therefore, the monopolistic practices of the meat-packers were not merely local transactions. The *Swift* case, the Chief Justice continued, controlled the *Stafford* decision. The doctrine in *Swift* had been so "clear and comprehensive" that it left to the Court in *Stafford* "little but the obvious application of the principles there developed." Praising *Swift* without mentioning *Knight*, Taft called Holmes's application of the Commerce Clause

the inevitable recognition of the great central fact that such streams of commerce from one part of the country to the other which are ever flowing are in their very essence the commerce among the states and with foreign nations which historically it was one of the chief purposes of the Constitution to bring under national protection and control.

The Chief Justice concluded his opinion by applying the reasonable doubt test to the act of Congress. "If Congress," Taft reasoned, "could provide for punishment or restraint of such conspiracies after their formation through the Anti-Trust Law as in the Swift Case, certainly it may provide regulation to prevent their formation." Furthermore, Congress's fear that unregulated local transactions would be used in "conspiracies" against interstate commerce was "reasonable," for "it is primarily for Congress to consider and decide the fact of danger [to interstate commerce] and meet it." "This Court," Taft emphasized, "will certainly not substitute its judgment for that of Congress in such a matter unless the relation of the subject to interstate commerce and its effect upon it are clearly nonexistent."

While *Stafford,* like *Swift,* did not specifically overrule *Knight,* it clearly seemed to leave little, if any, of the old doctrine standing. But so did *Swift,* and there had been *Hammer v. Dagenhart.* Still, Edward S. Corwin, writing in 1932, strongly believed, in view of *Swift* and *Stafford,* that the *Knight* doctrine was dead. Even "the proposition," he asserted, "that manufacturing is 'intrinsically' local, and so incapable . . . of affecting interstate commerce 'directly' . . . becomes a mere superstition— one of those judicial 'nevers' which seem to overlook how long a time *never* can be."[13]

If little of *Knight* seemed left after *Stafford,* little of *Lochner* seemed to survive after *Muller v. Oregon* (1908) and *Bunting v. Oregon* (1917). Only three years after *Lochner,* the Court in *Muller* unanimously upheld a ten-hour law for women. Justice Brewer attempted to distinguish the *Lochner* decision by insisting that inherent differences between the sexes justified protective legislation for women. Then in *Bunting* came the real break with *Lochner.* Justice McKenna's opinion for a narrow majority, upholding a ten-hour law with an overtime provision for men, neither overruled nor distinguished *Lochner;* instead, the Court simply ignored that precedent. The Oregon statute, McKenna held, was not "unreasonable" or "arbitrary," and, therefore, it did not violate the Fourteenth Amendment. The burden of proof had shifted from the state, where *Lochner* had misplaced it, back to those challenging the legislation, thereby restoring the traditional presumption of constitutionality.

But the unofficial interment of *Lochner* by *Bunting* was short-lived. Just as *Hammer* had resurrected the *Knight* doctrine after *Swift* had apparently disposed of it, so *Adkins v. Children's Hospital* (1923) unearthed the *Lochner* liberty of contract dogma only six years after *Bunting*. Congress in 1918 had sought to protect the standard of living of women and minor children in the District of Columbia by authorizing a board to set minimum wages for such workers, but the Court found the act in conflict with the Due Process Clause of the Fifth Amendment. Writing for the majority in *Adkins*, Justice Sutherland ignored *Bunting*, attempted to distinguish *Muller*, and, quoting extensively from Peckham's opinion in *Lochner*, invoked that decision as controlling precedent. As a result, a virtually absolute liberty of contract with respect to wage regulation was written into the Constitution, and a strong presumption of unconstitutionality was reattached to legislation affecting that freedom.

Perhaps to placate Felix Frankfurter, whose oral argument defending the act of Congress had leaned heavily on the reasonable doubt test, Justice Sutherland began his opinion by paying lip service to that standard and to the concomitant presumption of constitutionality. "This court," he wrote, "by an unbroken line of decisions from Chief Justice Marshall to the present day, has steadily adhered to the rule that every possible presumption is in favor of the validity of an act of Congress until overcome beyond rational doubt." Promising to hue to that venerable line of decisions, Sutherland quickly departed from it. "That the right to contract about one's affairs is a part of the liberty of the individual protected" by the Fifth Amendment, he noted, invoking *Lochner*, "is settled by the decisions of this Court and is no longer open to question." "There is, of course," Sutherland conceded, "no such thing as absolute freedom of contract." "But," he continued, "freedom of contract is, nevertheless, the general rule and restraint the exception; and the exercise of legislative authority to abridge it can be justified only by the existence of exceptional circumstances."

Having negated in one sentence what he had affirmed in the former, Sutherland proceeded to cope with precedents. *Lochner* alone was good authority; *Muller* was inapposite. In *Muller* the Court had upheld an hours, not a wage, regulation, and, mysteriously, the latter was the essential ingredient in a labor contract while the former was somehow insignificant. Hours of labor, he reasoned, had "no necessary effect upon the heart of the contract; that is, the amount of wages to be paid and received." "This court," the Justice stressed, "has been careful in every case where the question has been raised, to place its decision upon this limited authority of the legislature to regulate hours of labor and to disclaim any purpose to uphold the legislation as fixing wages, thus recognizing an essential difference between the two." Yet the ten-hour law upheld in *Bunting*, which Sutherland presumably considered strictly an hour regulation, included a provision that three additional hours might be worked at a time and one-half rate of pay, a stipulation hardly unrelated to wages. Sutherland concluded his opinion by exercising independent judgment to override Congress's determination that the health, welfare, and morals of women were related to their standard of living. "What is sufficient to supply the necessary cost of living for a woman worker and maintain her in good health and protect her morals," he opined, "is obviously not a precise or unvarying sum—not even approximately so." Because the relation between earnings and morals was "not capable of standardization," because it could not "be shown that well paid women safeguard their morals more carefully than those who are poorly paid," and because morality rested upon "other considerations than wages," it followed, Sutherland thought, that Congress was not justified in its "broad attempt to adjust [wages] with reference to [morals]."

Dissenting in *Adkins* were Chief Justice Taft and Justices Sanford and Holmes. All three agreed that the Court's reliance on *Lochner* was ill-founded, indeed, that *Bunting* had effectively overruled *Lochner*, and that the distinction between regulating maximum hours and minimum wages was clearly arbitrary, a distinction without a difference. It was "impossible" for Taft, joined by Sanford, to reconcile *Bunting* and *Lochner*, for Taft had "always supposed that the Lochner case was thus overruled *sub silentio*." Yet Sutherland's opinion in *Adkins*, the Chief Justice added, "quotes from the opinion in the Lochner Case as one which has been sometimes distinguished but never overruled. Certainly there was no attempt to distinguish it in the Bunting Case." Holmes concurred. After *Bunting*, he too "had supposed" that *Lochner* "would be allowed a deserved repose."

Because the majority opinion in *Adkins* did not overrule *Bunting*, Taft therefore assumed that the result in *Adkins* rested on the supposed distinction between minimum wages and maximum hours. Taft strongly disputed "the substance of this distinction." Each factor was "as important as the other, for both enter equally into the consideration given and received"; one factor is "the multiplier and the other the multiplicand." Holmes also could "not understand the principle on which the power to fix a minimum for the wages of women can be denied by those who admit the power to fix a maximum for their hours of work." "The bargain," he insisted, "is equally affected whichever half you regulate." Echoing his own dissent eighteen years earlier in *Lochner,* Holmes chastised the majority in *Adkins* for abandoning the reasonable doubt test and for rewriting into the Constitution "the dogma, Liberty of Contract."

Adkins thus served the same function as *Hammer v. Dagenhart.* Each kept alive a doctrine which had earlier been badly discredited but not expressly overruled. *Adkins* revived *Lochner,* which had been undercut by *Bunting,* just as *Hammer* restored *Knight,* which had been tarnished by *Swift.* The immediate impact of *Adkins,* however, was probably greater than that of *Hammer;* for while the latter was quickly attenuated by *Stafford v. Wallace, Adkins* was succeeded by a number of decisions which, without mentioning *Lochner,* testified to its continuing good health. In 1924, only two years after *Adkins,* the Court in *Jay Burns Baking Co. v. Bryan* struck down a Nebraska statute fixing the weight of loaves of bread to protect consumers against fraud and honest bakers from unfair competition. Brandeis, joined by Holmes, dissented and devoted over fourteen pages of his opinion to facts concerning the "art of bread-making" in order to demonstrate the reasonableness of the legislative determination. Even if the evidence supporting the legislative judgment were not conclusive, the legislature was still entitled to its viewpoint unless it could be shown to be clearly unreasonable. By substituting its independent judgment for a reasonable legislative judgment, the majority, Brandeis charged, had exercised "the powers of a super-legislature—not the performance of the constitutional function of judicial review." "Put at its highest," the dissenter lectured his colleagues in language reminiscent of Thayer, "our function is to determine ... whether the provision as applied is so clearly arbitrary or capricious that legislators acting reasonably could not have believed it to be necessary or appropriate for the public welfare."

Three years later, in *Tyson v. Banton* (1927), Brandeis and Holmes again dissented, as did Justice Stone. Justice Sutherland, writing for the majority, voided a New York law designed to protect the public against theater ticket scalpers by prohibiting the resale of tickets at no more than fifty cents above the original price. Sutherland conceded the existence of fraud, but, following *Adkins,* held that liberty of contract precluded the legislative remedy. "That such evils exist in some degree in connection with the theatrical business and its ally, the ticket broker, is," he wrote, "undoubtedly true," but they could not be cured by violating "essential rights of private property." This time it was Stone's turn to invoke Thayer's rule of administration. In an opinion joined by Brandeis and Holmes, Stone reminded the majority that protecting the consumer against fraud involved "considerations of economics about which there may be reasonable differences of opinion. Choice between these views," he added tersely, "takes us from the judicial to the legislative field."

Unimpressed, the Court continued to deprive state legislatures of choice between reasonable alternative policies. In *New State Ice Co. v. Liebmann,* decided in 1932, Justice Sutherland, again writing for the majority, struck down for violating the Due Process Clause an Oklahoma statute requiring a state license to manufacture ice for sale. While recognizing the fact of economic emergency and acknowledging that it "may be quite true that in Oklahoma ice is, not only an article of prime necessity, but indispensable," Sutherland was still "not able to see anything peculiar in the business here in question which distinguishes it from ordinary manufacture and production."

The dissenters, however, certainly could. Brandeis, joined by Stone, documented "the evil of destructive competition" in the ice business in Oklahoma. Many communities were often not supplied with ice at all, while many were oversupplied. The purpose of the licensing law, therefore, was simply to deny licenses where the necessity for another ice plant was absent and to encourage ice manufacturers to serve the state at large more adequately. The majority, Brandeis charged, had not only ignored the special experience of Oklahoma with respect to the ice business; it had also decided, in effect, that "the Federal Constitution confers an absolute right to engage anywhere in the business of manufacturing ice for sale." Repeating the accusation he had made in the *Jay Burns* case, Brandeis indicted the majority for acting like a "super-legislature," for erecting its own economic "prejudices into legal principles." "Our function," he cautioned, "is only to determine the reasonableness of the legislature's belief in the existence of evils and in the effectiveness of the remedy provided." Citing Thayer's famous article, "The Origin and Scope of the American Doctrine of Constitutional Law," Brandeis reiterated that the reasonable doubt test was the only legitimate standard of review: a legislative "determination is subject to judicial review; but the usual presumption of validity attends the enactment. The action of the state must be held valid unless clearly arbitrary, capricious or unreasonable."[14]

Over the strong dissents of Holmes, Brandeis, and Stone, the influence of *Lochner* seemed solidified not only by *Adkins* but also by its companion cases, *Jay Burns, Tyson,* and *Liebmann.* Yet only two years after *Liebmann* the Court appeared to switch tracks again when in *Nebbia v. New York,* decided in 1934, it sustained a state law fixing minimum and maximum milk prices. Speaking through Justice Roberts, the five-man majority now ignored the *Lochner-Adkins* line of precedent, which had all but enthroned liberty of contract, and instead applied the reasonable doubt test to the challenged legislation. Neither "property rights nor contract rights are absolute," Roberts wrote. "Equally fundamental with the private right is that of the public to regulate it in the common interest." "The Constitution," he pointed out, "does not guarantee the unrestricted privilege to engage in a business or to conduct it as one pleases."

Having put to rest the notion "that there is something peculiarly sacrosanct about the price one may charge for what he makes or sells" and having effectively restored the presumption of constitutionality, Roberts proceeded to measure due process by the reasonable doubt test. Due process, he stated, "demands only that the law shall not be unreasonable, arbitrary, or capricious, and that the means selected shall have a real and substantial relation to the object sought to be attained." Only if the law were "palpably in excess of legislative power" could the Court invalidate it. "With the wisdom of the policy adopted," Roberts concluded, "the courts are both incompetent and unauthorized to deal."[15]

By 1934, then, the development of economic due process in the Supreme Court had closely paralleled that of the Commerce Clause. Following an erratic path in each area, the Court had fashioned conflicting precedents. Yet on the eve of the Court's encounter with New Deal legislation in the mid-1930s, the most recent and presumably controlling precedents were *Nebbia,* regarding the Due Process Clause, and *Stafford,* regarding the Commerce Clause. Both augured well for the constitutional fate of the New Deal.[16] Then, in 1935–36, the Court changed directions again; *Knight* and *Lochner* had left enduring legacies.

The impact of *Knight* on the Court's decision in *Schechter v. United States* (1935), invalidating the National Industrial Recovery Act of 1933, was profound. Without actually citing the *Knight* case, Chief Justice Hughes, writing for a unanimous Court, revived both the dual federalism doctrine and the direct-indirect effects test in language that Chief Justice Fuller might have thought his own:

In determining how far the federal government may go in controlling intra-state transactions upon the ground that they "affect" interstate commerce, there is a necessary and well-established distinction between direct and indirect effects ... [which] must be recognized as a fundamental one, essential to the maintenance of our constitutional system. Otherwise ... there would be virtually no limit to the federal power, and for all practical purposes we should have a completely centralized government.[17]

It remained for Hughes to determine whether the effect on interstate commerce of wages, hours, and trade practices, local activities which Congress and the President had sought to regulate in an effort to restore national economic stability, was "direct" or "indirect." First, the Chief Justice rejected the *Swift-Stafford* precedents. The "stream of commerce" doctrine was inapt, Hughes thought, because the product here involved, live poultry, had reached its final resting place,[18] even though 96 percent of the live poultry sold in New York City, the nation's largest live-poultry market, came from out of state. Then Hughes rejected the Government's argument that the "final resting place" finding was irrelevant because the local activities still seriously and adversely affected commerce among the states. "The depressed state of the national economy," Government counsel had contended, "made it evident that interstate commerce was demoralized and endangered by acts which under other conditions might not seriously affect it." It followed that producing a desperately needed increase in national purchasing power depended in part upon regulating the wages and hours of all employees, including Schechters'.[19] To Hughes, however, this argument proved "too much." "If the commerce clause were construed to reach all enterprises and transactions which could be said to have an indirect effect upon interstate commerce," he reasoned in a manner reminiscent of Fuller in *Knight* and Day in *Dagenhart*, "the federal authority would embrace practically all the activities of the people, and the authority of the state over its domestic concerns would exist only by sufferance of the federal government." Where "the effect of intrastate transactions upon interstate commerce is merely indirect," the Chief Justice concluded, again linking the direct-indirect effects test to the dual federalism doctrine, "such transactions remain within the domain of state power."

So pervasive was the influence of the *Knight-Dagenhart* legacy that Justices Brandeis, Stone, and Cardozo were not yet ready to abandon it.[20] Their break came the next year, however, when the Court in *Carter v.*

Carter Coal Co. (1936) struck down the Bituminous Coal Conservation Act of 1935. Less timid, perhaps, than Chief Justice Hughes had been in *Schechter,* Justice Sutherland, writing for the majority in *Carter,* relied explicitly on *Dagenhart* and even quoted directly from Chief Justice Fuller's opinion in *Knight.* As in *Schechter,* dual federalism and the direct-indirect effects test controlled the Court's opinion, and the Guffey Coal Act, regulating coal prices and the hours and wages of coal miners, fell. The Government's position, persuasively put in oral argument,[21] that dual federalism was irrelevant, proved unavailing. It met with Sutherland's contention that "the plainest facts" emerging from the Constitutional Convention of 1787 and the state ratifying conventions clearly precluded the national government from exercising the kind of power embodied in the Guffey Coal Act. "It is safe to say," he wrote, "that if, when the Constitution was under consideration, it had been thought that any such danger [to states' rights] lurked behind its plain words, it would never have been ratified."[22]

The Government's other main argument, that the wages of coal miners had a substantial effect on interstate commerce especially because labor disputes resulting from wage-cutting had already interrupted, obstructed, and even threatened to halt interstate commerce in coal, was similarly received by the majority. Sutherland retorted that the magnitude of the effect was constitutionally unimportant. Recalling Fuller's statement that an indirect effect on interstate commerce, "however inevitable and whatever its extent," remained indirect and consequently unreachable by the national government, Sutherland proceeded further to define the direct-indirect effects test. He could not, indeed did not, deny the far-reaching effects of labor disputes in the coal industry on interstate commerce. Instead, Sutherland explained:

The word "direct" implies that the activity invoked or blamed shall operate proximately—not mediately, remotely, or collaterally—to produce the effect. It connotes the absence of an efficient intervening agency or condition. And the extent of the effect bears no logical relation to its character. The distinction between a direct and indirect effect turns, not upon the magnitude of either the cause or the effect, but entirely upon the manner in which the effect has been brought about.

Because a strike stops production, and the halting of production interferes with commerce among the states, it followed that the strike only indirectly affected interstate commerce—even though it might stop it completely. "Such effect," Sutherland declared, as labor disputes "may have upon commerce, however extensive it may be, is secondary and indirect. An increase in the greatness of the effect adds to its importance. It does not alter its character."

Justices Cardozo, Brandeis, and Stone had had enough.[23] Cardozo's opinion, joined by the other two dissenters, ever so gently rejected the direct-indirect effects test as defined and applied by the majority in *Carter* without appearing to disavow the position he had taken in *Schechter*. In his concurring opinion in *Schechter*, Cardozo had written: "The law is not indifferent to considerations of degree. Activities local in their immediacy do not become interstate and national because of distant repercussions." In *Carter*, however, Cardozo quoted only the first sentence of the *Schechter* passage:

Mining and agriculture and manufacture are not interstate commerce considered by themselves, yet their relation to that commerce may be such that for the protection of the one there is need to regulate the other. . . . Sometimes it is said that the relation must be "direct" to bring that power into play. In many circumstances such a description will be sufficiently precise to meet the needs of the occasion. But a great principle of constitutional law is not susceptible of comprehensive statement in an adjective. The underlying thought is merely this, that "the law is not indifferent to considerations of degree."

Having omitted the damaging qualifier, Cardozo further downgraded the direct-indirect effects test. Those words, "even if accepted as sufficient, must not," he warned, "be read too narrowly." Instead, they must be "interpreted with suppleness of adaptation and flexibility of meaning. The power is as broad as the need that invokes it." By paralyzing Congress's commerce power, the Court, Cardozo charged, had created a no-man's-land free from all regulation. Because the Court had earlier ruled that prices in interstate commerce "may not be regulated by the states," Cardozo thought that they "must therefore be subject to the power of the nation unless they are to be withdrawn altogether from governmental supervision." "If such a vacuum were permitted," the dissenter concluded, "many a public evil incidental to interstate transactions would be left without a remedy."

Thus, by 1936 the Court through the *Schechter* and *Carter* decisions had once again disinterred the *Knight-Dagenhart* doctrine, this time at the expense of the New Deal. Not surprisingly, the *Lochner-Adkins* doctrine also reemerged in 1936 when the Court in *Morehead v. New York ex. rel. Tipaldo* expressly reaffirmed the *Adkins* decision despite its more recent ruling in *Nebbia.* Writing for a five-man majority in *Morehead,* which invalidated New York's minimum wage law for women, Justice Butler relied specifically on *Adkins.* In his dissenting opinion, Chief Justice Hughes, who felt that *Adkins* need not be overruled, would have upheld the New York statute on the authority of *Nebbia* and *Muller.* Justice Stone, writing also for the other two dissenters, Justices Brandeis and Cardozo, insisted, like the majority, that *Adkins* was indistinguishable from *Morehead* and strongly implied that *Adkins* should be overruled because it was irreconcilable with *Nebbia.* Denouncing the liberty of contract dogma, Stone invoked the reasonable doubt test:

> The fact that at one time or another Congress and the legislatures of seventeen states, and the legislative bodies of twenty-one foreign countries ... have found that wage regulation is an appropriate corrective for serious social and economic maladjustments growing out of inequality of bargaining power, precludes, for me, any assumption that it is a remedy beyond the bounds of reason. It is difficult to imagine any grounds, other than our own personal predilections, for saying that the contract of employment is any the less an appropriate subject of legislation than are scores of others, in dealing with which this Court has held that legislatures may curtail individual freedom in the public interest.

Stone ended his dissent by paraphrasing Holmes in *Lochner:* The Fourteenth Amendment embodied a "particular set of economic beliefs" no more than it embodied "in the name of liberty, the system of theology which we may happen to approve."

Morehead, however, joined *Carter* as last hurrahs in the Court's effort to block economic regulation at both state and national levels. Barely ten months after *Morehead,* the first stage of the Court "revolution" of 1937 began when in *West Coast Hotel Co. v. Parrish* Justice Roberts parted company with Justices Sutherland, McReynolds, Van Devanter, and Butler and sided with Chief Justice Hughes and Justices Brandeis, Stone, and Cardozo in overruling both *Morehead* and *Adkins.* Now holding that statutes, both state and national, prescribing minimum wages for women and minors, did not violate liberty of contract, the Chief Justice, speaking for the newly formed majority, applied the reasonable doubt test, rediscovered *Bunting,* and extolled the dissenting opinions of Holmes and Taft in *Adkins.* The decision in *Adkins,* Hughes noted, had been an aberration, "a departure from the true application of the principles governing the regulation by the state of employer and employed."

Then came *National Labor Relations Board v. Jones & Laughlin Steel Corporation* and the beginning of the end of *Carter.* Handed down only two weeks after *Parrish,* the Court's decision in *Jones & Laughlin* upheld the National Labor Relations Act of 1935; but the Chief Justice's opinion of the Court, which divided just as it had in *Parrish,* was a masterpiece of ambiguity, as bifurcated probably as the Court's entire treatment of the Commerce Clause had been since 1895. The four dissenters, speaking through Justice McReynolds, were surely correct in urging that if *Schechter* and *Carter* were still controlling, then the National Labor Relations Act should fall; its labor relations sections were substantially the same as those of the Guffey Coal Act. Yet for Hughes and the majority in *Jones & Laughlin,* the *Schechter* and *Carter* cases were, incredibly, "not controlling here."

The Chief Justice's opinion in *Schechter* seems designed both to uphold congressional power in this particular case and to preserve the old *Knight-Dagenhart* principles, possibly for future revival. Thus, Hughes implicitly rejected the *Knight* case as precedent and explicitly rejected the notion, so vital in *Knight* and *Dagenhart* as well as in Hughes's own opinions in *Schechter* and *Carter,* that because commerce succeeds to manufacture, the latter is beyond the purview of Congress's commerce power. That "the employees here concerned were engaged in production," he wrote in *Jones & Laughlin,* "is not determinative." Yet *Schechter* was twice invoked by Hughes to give continuing content to "the explicit reservation of the Tenth Amendment," which was intended to preserve "our dual system of government" against attempts to "obliterate the distinction between what is national and what is local and create a completely centralized government." On the other hand, the Chief Justice paid homage to the reasonable doubt test, and he even twice found the *Stafford* precedent, which he had attempted to distinguish in *Schechter* and had ignored in *Carter,* now surprisingly relevant.

Then Hughes reached the crucial issue, whether the labor practices in the Jones & Laughlin Steel Corporation affected interstate commerce in such a manner as to justify congressional regulation. While asserting that the local activities both directly and severely affected interstate commerce, the Chief Justice seemed nevertheless to abandon the requirement that the effect be direct, so long as it was sufficiently severe:

[T]he fact remains that the stoppage of those [local] operations by industrial strife would have a most serious effect upon interstate commerce. In view of [Jones & Laughlin's] far-flung activities, it is idle to say that the effect would be indirect or remote. It is obvious that it would be immediate and might be catastrophic. We are asked to shut our eyes to the plainest facts of our national life and to deal with the question of direct and indirect effects in an intellectual vacuum. . . . When industries organize themselves on a national scale, making their relation to interstate commerce the dominant factor in their activities, how can it be maintained that their industrial labor relations constitute a forbidden field into which Congress may not enter when it is necessary to protect commerce from the paralyzing consequences of industrial war? We have often said that interstate commerce itself is a practical conception. It is equally true that interferences with that commerce must be appraised by a judgment that does not ignore actual experience.[24]

The dismayed dissenters in *Jones & Laughlin* were left, as they had been in *Parrish*, to repeat themselves. Relying on *Knight* and invoking the Tenth Amendment, which was supposed to put the "indestructible powers" of the states "beyond controversy," they accused the majority of discarding the direct-indirect effects test which, if applied as it had been in *Schechter* and *Carter*, would have rendered the National Labor Relations Act unconstitutional.

If any hope lingered after *Jones & Laughlin* for the restoration of the direct-indirect effects test and the dual federalism doctrine, it was soon dashed when a unanimous Court in *United States v. Darby* (1941) and in *Wickard v. Filburn* (1942) struck the death knell for the *Knight-Dagenhart* offspring. In upholding the Fair Labor Standards Act of 1938, which fixed minimum wages and maximum hours for producers of goods shipped in interstate commerce, the Court in *Darby,* speaking through Justice Stone instead of Chief Justice Hughes, who silently joined the opinion, squarely overruled *Hammer v. Dagenhart.* That case, Stone said in a style resembling Hughes's treatment in *Parrish* of *Adkins v. Children's Hospital,* "was a departure from the principles which have prevailed in the interpretation of the commerce clause both before and since the decision and . . . such vitality, as a precedent, as it then had has long since been exhausted." Elevated to its proper status was "the powerful and now classic dissent of Mr. Justice Holmes" in *Dagenhart,* and correctly interpreted was Marshall's opinion in the leading case of *Gibbons v. Ogden.* "So far as *Carter v. Carter Coal Co. . . .* is inconsistent" with the conclusions reached in *Darby*, Stone added, "its doctrine is limited in principle by the decisions under the Sherman Act and the National Labor Relations Act." "Our conclusions," the Chief Justice soon-to-be emphasized, putting the doctrine of dual federalism to rest, "is unaffected by the Tenth Amendment, which . . . states but a truism that all is retained which has not been surrendered."

As if for good measure, the Court in *Wickard* finally disposed conclusively of the direct-indirect effects test. In sustaining the Agricultural Adjustment Act of 1938, which regulated the production of wheat even when not intended for interstate commerce but wholly for consumption on the producer's farm, a unanimous Court, speaking through Justice Jackson, declared that "questions of the power of Congress [under the Commerce Clause] are not to be decided by reference to any formula which would give controlling force to nomenclature such as 'production' and 'indirect' and foreclose consideration of the actual effects of the activity in question upon interstate commerce." The "mechanical application of legal formulas," he went on, is "no longer feasible. Once an economic measure of the reach of the power granted to Congress in the Commerce Clause is accepted, questions of federal power cannot be decided simply by finding the activity in question to be 'production,' nor can consideration of its economic effects be foreclosed by calling them 'indirect.'" Instead, Jackson explained, a local activity, "whatever its nature," may "be reached by Congress if it exerts a substantial effect on interstate commerce and this irrespective of whether such effect is what might at some earlier time have been defined as 'direct' or 'indirect.'" Like Stone in *Darby*, Jackson in *Wickard* returned "to the principles first enunciated by Chief Justice Marshall in *Gibbons v. Ogden.*"

By 1942, then, the Court had finally come full circle. The direct-indirect effects test and the doctrine of dual federalism at last went the way of the liberty of contract dogma. But it had been a long and tortuous journey, for the so-called "switch in time" was actually the last in a series of switches spanning over four decades. Like *Lochner* and *Adkins, Knight* and *Dagenhart* had been difficult precedents to overcome.[25] During the period between 1895 and 1936, the reasonable doubt test had often been ignored, inverted, and otherwise misapplied, all in the service of property rights and states' rights. A similar exercise of independent judicial judgment, this time on behalf of nonproperty rights, would recur under the Warren Court. But first a doctrinal justification for the "preferred" status to be accorded certain non-property rights would emerge.

4

FOOTNOTE FOUR AND
PREFERRED FREEDOMS

A ready-made rationale for the exercise of independent judicial judgment in areas allegedly having preferred constitutional status preceded Earl Warren's accession to the Chief Justiceship. Famous footnote four, a three-paragraph addendum to Justice Harlan Fiske Stone's opinion of the Court in *United States v. Carolene Products Co.* (1938), would provide much of the doctrinal support. Written during the Court's transition from judicial supremacy in the service of property rights to the same role in the service of nonproperty rights, the opinion explicitly affirmed that the reasonable doubt test would henceforth be applied to legislative regulation of the economy. Upholding congressional prohibition of the shipment of filled milk in interstate commerce on the ground that Congress could reasonably have believed such milk was injurious to health and a fraud on the public, Stone emphasized that regulatory legislation affecting ordinary commercial transactions would generally be assumed to rest upon some rational basis within the knowledge and experience of the legislators. Then came the footnote:

There may be narrower scope for operation of the presumption of constitutionality when legislation appears on its face to be within a specific prohibition of the Constitution, such as those of the first ten amendments, which are deemed equally specific when held to be embraced within the Fourteenth. See *Stromberg v. California,* 283 U.S. 359, 369–370; *Lovell v. Griffin,* 303 U.S. 444, 452.

It is unnecessary to consider now whether legislation which restricts those political processes which can ordinarily be expected to bring about repeal of undesirable legislation, is to be subjected to more exacting judicial scrutiny under the general prohibitions of the Fourteenth Amendment than are most other types of legislation. On restrictions upon the right to vote, see *Nixon v. Herndon*, 273 U.S. 536; *Nixon v. Condon*, 286 U.S. 73; on restraints upon dissemination of information, see *Near v. Minnesota ex rel. Olson*, 283 U.S. 697, 713-714, 718-720, 722; *Grosjean v. American Press Co.*, 297 U.S. 233; *Lovell v. Griffin, supra;* on interferences with political organizations, see *Stromberg v. California, supra* 369; *Fiske v. Kansas*, 274 U.S. 380; *Whitney v. California*, 274 U.S. 357, 373-378; *Herndon v. Lowry*, 301 U.S. 242; and see Holmes, J., in *Gitlow v. New York*, 268 U.S. 652, 673; as to prohibition of peaceable assembly, see *DeJonge v. Oregon*, 299 U.S. 353, 365.

Nor need we enquire whether similar considerations enter into the review of statutes directed at particular religious, *Pierce v. Society of Sisters*, 268 U.S. 510, or national, *Meyer v. Nebraska*, 262 U.S. 390; *Bartels v. Iowa*, 262 U.S. 404; *Farrington v. Tokushige*, 273 U.S. 284, or racial minorities, *Nixon v. Herndon, supra; Nixon v. Condon, supra:* whether prejudice against discrete and insular minorities may be a special condition, which tends seriously to curtail the operation of those political processes ordinarily to be relied upon to protect minorities, and which may call for a correspondingly more searching judicial inquiry. Compare *McCulloch v. Maryland*, 4 Wheat. 316, 428; *South Carolina v. Barnwell Bros.*, 303 U.S. 177, 184 n.2, and cases cited.

Without even attempting to explain why property rights deserved less judicial protection than nonproperty rights,[1] Stone asserted that special judicial scrutiny—involving a reversal of the traditional presumption of constitutionality[2] and thereby permitting the exercise of independent judicial judgment—might be required when First Amendment freedoms are allegedly infringed, when the rights of racial, religious, or national minorities are allegedly violated, or when the political process itself is allegedly impeded. Laying claim to judicial supremacy in behalf of what was later dubbed "preferred freedoms,"[3] the footnote relied heavily on such venerable and imposing authority as certain opinions of Chief Justice Marshall, Justices Holmes, Brandeis, Cardozo, and the then Chief Justice, Charles Evans Hughes. The problem, however, is that these opinions, while affirming the *importance* of First Amendment freedoms, the rights of certain minorities, and an unimpeded political process, lend little support to Stone's suggestion that legislation that allegedly adversely affects rights in these areas might legitimately be subject to a reversal of the presumption of constitutionality; nor do these opinions imply that nonproperty rights are more important than property rights.

The first paragraph of footnote four refers to *Stromberg v. California* (1931) and *Lovell v. Griffin* (1938), both opinions of the Court written by Chief Justice Hughes that involve no reversal of the presumption of constitutionality and provide no basis for the preferred freedoms doctrine. *Stromberg* simply struck down a state law prohibiting the display of a red flag "as a sign, symbol, or emblem of opposition to organized government" on the ground that it violated freedom of speech as protected by the Fourteenth Amendment; the statute could clearly be construed, the Court held, as embracing conduct that the state could not constitutionally prohibit, i.e., peaceful and orderly opposition to government by constitutionally protected means. *Lovell* invalidated a city ordinance barring the distribution of any kind of literature without a permit as clearly a prior restraint on freedom of speech and of the press; *Near v. Minnesota* (1931) was the controlling precedent. Both *Stromberg* and *Lovell* involved legislation the Court found clearly unconstitutional "on its face," and *Stromberg* stressed that enjoyment of First Amendment freedoms was a prerequisite to participation in the political process. But neither decision reversed the presumption of constitutionality or indicated that First Amendment freedoms held preferred constitutional status.[4]

In the second paragraph of footnote four, the references to opinions condemning unconstitutional restrictions on the political process likewise give no support to Stone's inferences. In fact, Holmes's opinion in *Nixon v. Herndon* (1927), in which a unanimous Court struck down a Texas statute forbidding Negroes the right to vote in the Democratic party primary election, twice invoked the reasonable doubt test as the controlling judicial standard. Holding that the law violated the Equal Protection Clause of the Fourteenth Amendment, Holmes wrote: "the answer does not seem to us open to a doubt"; "it is too clear for extended argument that color cannot be made the basis of a statutory classification" affecting the right to vote. Relying on *Herndon,* Cardozo's opinion of the Court in *Nixon v. Condon* (1932) invalidated a similar resolution by the State Executive Committee of the Texas Democratic party acting under authority of statute. Neither opinion accorded preferred status to rights relating to the political process.[5] Even Brandeis's famous concurring opinion, joined by Holmes, in *Whitney v. California* (1927),[6] in which the Court upheld a conviction for advocating unlawful force in violation of a state Criminal Syndicalism Act, disavows rather than supports the notion of preferred freedoms. The power of the courts to strike down an offending law, Brandeis said, is "no less when the interests involved are not property rights, but the fundamental personal rights of free speech and assembly." Despite Brandeis's strong affirmation that First Amendment freedoms are crucial to the political process, he did not suggest that judicial power to protect these rights was any greater than judicial power to protect property rights. Indeed, both Brandeis and Holmes upheld Miss Whitney's conviction on the basis of the reasonable doubt test. Both thought that a trial court or jury could reasonably have found that her activity constituted a "clear and present danger" to the security of the state, and both accordingly refused to exercise independent judgment to overrule the verdict.

Stone's references in the third paragraph of footnote four to opinions invalidating legislation prejudicial to minorities suffer from the same defects. McReynolds's opinion of the Court in *Pierce v. Society of Sisters* (1925), holding an Oregon law requiring compulsory public school education unconstitutional as a violation of the liberty of parents and guardians to direct the education of children under their control, neither reverses the presumption of constitutionality nor embodies any suggestion of preferred freedoms. Furthermore, the opinion relies heavily on *Meyer v. Nebraska* (1923), Stone's other reference, in which McReynolds's opinion of the Court twice invoked the reasonable doubt test to strike down a state law forbidding the teaching of any modern language other than English to any pupil who had not passed the eighth grade. Knowledge by a child of some language other than English was not "so clearly harmful," McReynolds held, as to justify the plain interference with the right of a foreign language teacher to teach and the right of parents to engage him to instruct their children. It should also be noted that Holmes, joined by Sutherland, dissented in *Meyer* on the express ground that, in their opinion, the statute was saved by the reasonable doubt test. Appealing to the test three times, Holmes was "not prepared to say that it is unreasonable" to provide that a child shall hear and speak only English at school, especially if there were areas of the state where he would hear only a foreign language at home. While Holmes appreciated the objection to the law, it nevertheless presented to him "a question upon which men reasonably might differ."

The third paragraph of footnote four closes with reference to the authority of John Marshall in *McCulloch v. Maryland*, where the Chief Justice repudiated the suggestion that every argument that would sustain the right of the national government to tax banks chartered by the states would equally sustain state taxation of national instrumentalities. The analogy did not stand up, as Marshall explained:

The people of all the states have created the general government, and have conferred upon it the general power of taxation. The people of all the states, and the states themselves, are represented in Congress, and, by their representatives, exercise this power. When they tax the chartered institutions of the states, they tax their constituents. . . . But when a state taxes the operations of the government of the United States, it acts upon institutions created, not by their own constituents, but by people over whom they claim no control. It acts upon the measures of a government created by others as well as themselves, for the benefit of others in common with themselves. The difference is that which always exists, and always must exist, between the action of the whole on a part, and the action of a part on the whole—between the laws of a government declared to be supreme, and those of a government which, when in opposition to those laws, is not supreme.[7]

Marshall's statement, thought by some students of the Court to be Stone's most impressive doctrinal support for the ideas contained in both paragraphs two and three,[8] suggested to Stone that the Court might have a special duty to correct the outcome of an impeded political process, as in the case of state taxation of national instrumentalities, when political restraints on state action were not available,[9] and furthermore that the Court might have a similar duty to purify the political process so as to minimize dependence on a judicial remedy.[10] According to Louis Lusky, once Stone's law clerk and believed to be part-author of the footnote,[11] the last two paragraphs embody

a frank recognition that the Court feels special responsibility for the protection of the "political processes," because, unless some non-political agency intervenes, interferences with the collective mechanism may well perpetuate themselves. The Court thus performs an important part in the maintenance of the basic conditions of just legislation. By preserving the hope that bad laws can and will be changed, the Court preserves the basis for the technique of political obligation, minimizing extra-legal opposition to the government by making it unnecessary. . . . Where the regular corrective processes are interfered with, the Court must remove the interference; where the dislike of minorities renders those processes ineffective to accomplish their underlying purpose of holding out a real hope that unwise laws will be changed, the Court itself must step in.[12]

Marshall's dictum in *McCulloch*, however, implied nothing of the sort. Quite unnecessary to the disposition of the second issue in the case, whether Maryland could constitutionally tax the United States Bank, because application of the Supremacy Clause had already resolved the issue, Marshall's observation was simply his own justification of the doctrine of national supremacy contained in the Supremacy Clause. An argument for the supremacy of the constitutional outcome of the national political process over the conflicting outcome of any state's political process, it implied nothing about the purity of *either* political process; still less did it suggest a special judicial duty to revise the constitutional outcome of either political process in the service of a more desirable outcome or a special judicial duty to remove constitutionally imposed or constitutionally permitted antidemocratic impediments to the pure functioning of either political process. For the issue in *McCulloch* was *which* political process, however pure or impure, democratic or antidemocratic, was constitutionally entitled to prevail. That the national political process emerged triumphant was, of course, in part a function of Marshall's belief that the action of the state of Maryland was, from the perspective of non-Marylanders, grossly undemocratic, tantamount to taxation without representation, for patently only Marylanders participated in the decision to tax the national bank. But the corrective did not depend on Marshall's belief that Maryland had acted undemocratically; the Supremacy Clause clearly provided, indeed required,[13] constitutional relief.

Marshall's decision in *McCulloch*, then, did not suggest a judicial duty to purify the political process. As is well known, all political processes affected by that decision, the national political system as well as those of the states, were constitutionally less than purely democratic, and intentionally so. Just as all inhabitants of the United States could not constitutionally participate, even indirectly, in the decision-making process that resulted in the establishment of the United States Bank, so all Marylanders could not constitutionally participate, even indirectly, in the decision to tax the bank; and those who could constitutionally participate in either decision-making process obviously could not constitutionally exert equal influence on its outcome. For a whole bevy of constitutional devices, among them, federalism, separation of powers, bicameral legislatures, the presidential veto, nonpopular representation in the Senate, restrictions on suffrage—all motivated, in varying degrees, by a fear of unrestrained majority rule and by a reaction to the so-called "excess of democracy"[14]—had been purposely designed to impede the democratic operation of the political process.[15]

Scantily supported, therefore, by the references Stone invoked, footnote four suffers additionally from serious logical deficiencies. For example, the dubious distinction drawn in paragraph one between the scope of judicial protection for property rights as opposed to nonproperty rights, retaining the reasonable doubt test for the review of legislation allegedly infringing the former but implying a reversal of the presumption of constitutionality when legislation "appears on its face" to infringe the latter, runs smack into George D. Braden's cogent objection:

[L]egislation not within a "specific" prohibition of the Constitution could still "appear on its face" to be invalid and would be so declared, as for example, an act of Congress purporting to regulate "commerce not interstate or affecting such," or a state statute which purported to take property from A and give it to B simply because the legislators disliked A.[16]

A curious logic also pervades paragraphs two and three. The suggestion that because a "dependence on the people" through the political process is, as James Madison put it, the "primary control" on government, the Court, as an "auxiliary" check, therefore has a special duty to undo the undesirable outcome of an impure political process, and even to purify an impure political process, either conveniently ignores the constitutionally intended antidemocratic nature of the political process or implies that the Court should rewrite the Constitution. The political process argument, then, proves either too little or too much: too little since it begs the question why the Court should exercise its independent judgment to determine the character of the political process and of its outcome when the Constitution prescribes its own procedures for change, and when, moreover, reasonable men surely differ over the desired scope of political and social democracy;[17] too much since the political process argument alone might well logically justify the judicial excision from the American political system of such antimajoritarian, yet clearly constitutional, institutions as the United States Senate, the Electoral College, even the Supreme Court itself.

The suggestion in paragraph two that because First Amendment freedoms are indispensable to effective participation in the political process they therefore deserve special judicial protection, even beyond their clear constitutional scope, likewise begs the question why the Court should exercise independent judgment to enlarge First Amendment freedoms in accordance with the Court's determination of the desired relationship between those freedoms and the political process. After all, to the extent that First Amendment freedoms, or any other freedoms, *are* clearly protected constitutionally, their judicial enforcement does not depend on the political process argument any more than did Marshall's invalidation of the Maryland tax in *McCulloch*. Moreover, to the extent that such freedoms are *not* clearly protected constitutionally, the justification for judicial expansion, or contraction, of their scope depends on whether the Court is empowered to rewrite the Constitution in the service of judicially desired constitutional change.

Finally, the corollary suggestion in paragraphs two and three that the Court has a special duty to enable particular "discrete and insular" minorities, vulnerable to majoritarian prejudice, to undo or attempt to undo undesirable legislation through the political process, involves similar logical difficulties. Why, for example, only religious, national, and racial minorities? Why not economic minority groups, too?[18] As Robert A. Dahl has effectively demonstrated, the passage of all legislation normally requires a coalition of various minorities which then prevail over other minorities.[19] Why, then, should any minority that loses in the political process, but that has not had any constitutional rights clearly infringed, enjoy an appeal to the judicial process either to expand those constitutional rights which affect participation in the political process or to reverse the outcome of that process? Plainly, whatever the nature of the political process, however unimpeded, minorities inevitably lose, in the sense of not prevailing politically. Given, therefore, a political system in which, for example, all members of the body politic could exert equal influence on the decision-making processes, would the losing minorities still deserve special protection beyond judicial enforcement of clear constitutional guarantees?

Perhaps so, defenders of footnote four suggest; for they argue that for the sake of peaceful societal change, instead of violent revolution, all minorities must be able to believe that the political process truly permits the repeal of "undesirable" legislation and that, consequently, judicial review, exercised for this purpose, becomes a surrogate for revolution.[20] To recognize, however, that judicial enforcement of Bill of Rights limitations on government would be a valuable aid in helping to domesticate revolution is not to concede a broad scope for judicial judgment.[21] Nor does it follow that the judiciary has a special duty to undo the allegedly undesirable, albeit constitutional, outcome of the political process simply because a disgruntled minority fought the good battle and lost. For what of the potentially even more disgruntled majority that also fought the good battle in the political process only to have its hard-won victory, obtained without any clear violation of the constitutional rights of the minority, upset in the judicial process? Such a majority, or as Dahl would have it, a transiently united group of minorities, might well have more cause than the defeated minority, now victorious in the judicial process, to be impatient with the likelihood of getting peaceful change through either the political or the judicial processes. Furthermore, why should a minority's view of desirable legislation prevail in the judicial process over a majority's constitutional right to choose in the political process a different policy, thought by a minority to be merely "undesirable"? Indeed, why should the Court have any call to invalidate so-called undesirable legislation over which reasonable men regularly and justifiably disagree?

At bottom, then, footnote four contained suggestions lacking in authority and logic and thoroughly incompatible with the traditional scope of judicial review as articulated by James Bradley Thayer. Not surprisingly, the influence of the footnote was quickly felt by both Court and country. Barely two years after it was written, footnote four divided the Court in *Minersville v. Gobitis,* in which Justice Frankfurter, writing for the Court with only Justice Stone dissenting, upheld state power to require the flag salute of children in public schools in violation of the religious scruples of Jehovah's Witnesses. Three years later when the Court reversed itself in *West Virginia v. Barnette,* Frankfurter was a dissenter and Stone, now Chief Justice, joined in Justice Jackson's majority opinion.

Stone and Jackson, urging the unconstitutionality of the flag salute requirement, eschewed the political process argument so prominent in footnote four. The argument was irrelevant, they thought, for participation of minorities in the political process did not thereby render their constitutional rights subject to the will of the majority; however democratic the political process might be, judicially enforceable constitutional limitations would prevail. Accordingly, Stone and Jackson relied strongly on other facets of footnote four: the fact that Jehovah's Witnesses were not only a minority but also a small religious minority; their belief that

First Amendment freedoms, which Jackson expressly accorded preferred constitutional status, were infringed; and their willingness to exercise independent judicial judgment in behalf of preferred freedoms. Frankfurter, however, found the political process argument quite relevant; it was for him the core of footnote four. But precisely because the Jehovah's Witnesses were not excluded from the political process and were free to oppose the flag salute requirement, Frankfurter thought the political process argument unavailing. Like Stone and Jackson, then, Frankfurter apparently would have voted to strike down unconstitutional obstructions of the political process, but unlike his colleagues Frankfurter rejected the constitutional relevance of the Jehovah's Witnesses' status as a small minority and refused to exercise independent judgment in behalf of preferred freedoms. That the Jehovah's Witnesses were a religious group was, of course, constitutionally relevant to Frankfurter, but the only issue for him was whether, according to the reasonable doubt test, the flag salute requirement violated their free exercise of religion.

What really divided Stone and Frankfurter in the first *Flag Salute* case, then, was not the political process argument but the legitimate scope of judicial review. The political process argument was inapplicable, Frankfurter urged, because "the remedial channels of the democratic process" were "open and unobstructed"; "all the effective means of inducing political changes" were free from interference. Stone agreed, but he was not persuaded that the Court "should refrain from passing upon the legislative judgment" simply because the political process was unimpeded. Such restraint seemed to Stone "no more than the surrender of the constitutional protection of the liberty of small minorities to the popular will." Implying, at least to Frankfurter, that the exercise of independent judicial judgment was appropriate in this case, Stone concluded that the flag salute requirement operated "to repress the religious freedom of small minorities."

Twice rejecting the independent judgment test in his opinion of the Court, and again in a letter to Stone,[22] Frankfurter instead applied the reasonable doubt test. "The mere possession of religious convictions which contradict the relevant concerns of a political society," he held, "does not relieve the citizen from the discharge of political responsibilities." Surely, Frankfurter thought, the legislative end—the promotion of good citizenship and patriotism—was legitimate; the crucial question was whether the means, however unwise, were irrational. The issue, he

concluded, was highly debatable, for the means for attaining the legislative end were "still so uncertain and so unauthenticated by science as to
preclude us from putting the widely prevalent belief in flag-saluting
beyond the pale of legislative power." The "wisdom of training children
in patriotic impulses," Frankfurter believed, "is not for our independent
judgment. Even were we convinced of the folly of such a measure, such
belief would be no proof of its unconstitutionality."

Any doubt over the real rift between Stone and Frankfurter in *Gobitis*
disappeared when Jackson, speaking for the Court in the second *Flag
Salute* case, explicitly affirmed the implications of Stone's earlier dissent.
Again the political process argument did not divide the justices; rather,
Jackson's categorical insistence on the Court's special duty to exercise
independent judgment in the service of preferred freedoms provoked
Frankfurter's strident dissent. Rejecting the relevance of the political
process argument, Jackson pointed out that the "very purpose of a Bill
of Rights was to withdraw certain subjects from the vicissitudes of political controversy." These rights, he added, "may not be submitted to vote;
they depend on the outcome of no election." Certain of these rights,
moreover, deserved greater judicial protection than others:

The right of a State to regulate, for example, a public utility may well
include, so far as the due process test is concerned, power to impose all
of the restrictions which a legislature may have a "rational basis" for
adopting. But freedoms of speech and of press, of assembly, and of wor-
ship may not be infringed on such slender grounds. They are susceptible
of restriction only to prevent grave and immediate danger to interests
which the State may lawfully protect.

The "*laissez-faire* concept or principle of noninterference has withered
at least as to economic affairs," Jackson believed, and "changed conditions" had thrust upon the justices necessary reliance "upon our own
judgment" in enforcing such nonproperty rights as First Amendment
freedoms. However doubtful the alleged violation of First Amendment
freedoms, however much reasonable men might differ over the issue,
the presumption of constitutionality in favor of legislation allegedly infringing those freedoms, but not legislation allegedly infringing property
rights, was, as Jackson wrote shortly before joining the Court,
"frankly reversed."[23] Justice Jackson concluded in *Barnette* that the
Court had an unwelcome duty, earned not by any marked "competence"

but imposed "by force of our commissions," to exercise independent judgment in behalf of preferred freedoms.

To Justice Frankfurter, neither history nor changed conditions regarding increased governmental regulation of property rights, nor especially the force of his commission, implied any such duty. Inveighing against the Court's rejection of the reasonable doubt test in favor of the exercise of independent judgment, he lamented that he knew of no standard other than the reasonable doubt test "which this Court is authorized to apply in nullifying legislation." The only issue properly before the Court, he urged, was "our opinion whether legislators could in reason have enacted such a law." But the Court had demanded more than a rational basis for the flag salute requirement; by exercising its own independent judgment, the Court had denied state legislatures their independent judgment between alternative rational means for attaining a legitimate legislative end:

We are told that a flag salute is a doubtful substitute for adequate understanding of our institutions. The states that require such a school exercise do not have to justify it as the only means for promoting good citizenship in children, but merely as one of diverse means for accomplishing a worthy end. We may deem it a foolish measure, but the point is that this Court is not the organ of government to resolve doubts as to whether it will fulfill its purpose. Only if there be no doubt that any reasonable mind could entertain can we deny to the states the right to resolve doubts their way and not ours.

By exercising independent judgment in behalf of preferred freedoms the Court, Frankfurter thought, had upended the historic meaning of the religious freedom protected by the First Amendment; it had created an "exceptional immunity from civic measures of general applicability." The constitutional protection of religious freedom, according to Frankfurter's reading of history,

terminated disabilities, it did not create new privileges. It gave religious equality, not civil immunity. Its essence is freedom from conformity to religious dogma, not freedom from conformity to law because of religious dogma. Otherwise, each individual could set up his own censor against obedience to laws conscientiously deemed for the public good by those whose business it is to make laws.

Not only had the Court distorted the intended constitutional relationship between religious freedom and political obligation; it had also distorted,

Frankfurter argued, the intended constitutional relationship between majority rule and minority rights. By attaching unwarranted significance to the fact that Jehovah's Witnesses were a small minority, the Court had, in effect, lost sight of the truism that the right to participate in the political process did not imply the right to prevail; that while the majority is limited by the right of minorities peacefully to oppose, the majority has a right to prevail so long as its choice is not clearly unconstitutional. Because the Jehovah's Witnesses were not barred access to the political process, and all channels of affirmative free expression remained open to them "to disavow as publicly as they choose to do so the meaning that others attach to the gesture of a salute," their status as a losing minority in the political process was, Frankfurter insisted, constitutionally irrelevant; their claim could rest only on a clear violation of their religious freedom. But as "no inroads" were made upon "the actual exercise of religion by the minority," Frankfurter concluded that "to deny the political power of the majority to enact laws concerned with civil matters, simply because they may offend the consciences of a minority, really means that the consciences of a minority are more sacred and more enshrined in the Constitution than the consciences of a majority."

Justice Frankfurter ended his long dissent in *Barnette* by quoting extensively from James Bradley Thayer, whose thesis, Frankfurter observed, was "as wise as any that I knew in analyzing what is really involved when the theory of this Court's function is put to the test of practice." Frankfurter's plea for judicial restraint—for application of the reasonable doubt test—went unheeded by the Court in *Barnette*. With the "casualness of a footnote," as Frankfurter once regretted,[24] Justice Stone in the *Carolene Products* case had suggested a rationale for judicial supremacy—for the exercise of independent judicial judgment in the service of preferred freedoms, the rights of certain minorities, and of a purified political process. Adopted by the Court in Justice Jackson's opinion in the second *Flag Salute* case, that rationale would flower, even flourish, under the Warren Court.

5

THE WARREN COURT AND THE
EXERCISE OF INDEPENDENT JUDGMENT
IN BEHALF OF PREFERRED FREEDOMS

At long last John Marshall, universally recognized as "the great Chief Justice," seems to have a serious rival for that accolade. Earl Warren, the fourteenth Chief Justice, who headed the Court from 1953 to 1969, barely half of Marshall's tenure, has been favorably compared with the fourth Chief Justice. Even before Warren's retirement, distinguished students of the Court began to rank him with Marshall. "I have thought for some years," U.S. District Court Judge Charles E. Wyzanski, Jr. professed in 1967, "that Chief Justice Warren will go down in history second only to Chief Justice Marshall." Wyzanski's appraisal rested, however, not on Warren's "intellect, legal acumen, style, or personal ascendancy" but rather on his "insight as to the central purposes and potentialities of the society in which he functioned" and on his "capacity to make the judicial power a chief instrument for their realization."[1] Warren would hardly have disagreed; for implicit in Wyzanski's evaluation is the widely held belief that judicial review necessarily and properly requires judicial statesmanship, and Warren would hardly have denied that the attempt to fashion wise public policy was the hallmark of the Warren Court.

The late Chief Justice more than once obligingly identified what he considered the most important decisions of his Court; he also articulated the political philosophy behind them. In a news conference held on July 5, 1968, Warren proudly acclaimed the reapportionment decisions of *Baker v. Carr* in 1962, and *Wesberry v. Sanders* and *Reynolds v. Sims* in 1964, as his Court's major contribution to the solution of the problems that confronted America. Many of these problems, he noted, without naming them, "could have been disposed of earlier if the legislatures had been properly apportioned before the Supreme Court required it." Next in importance Warren cited *Brown v. Board of Education,* the school de-segregation decision of 1954, and third on his list was *Gideon v. Wain-wright,* decided in 1963, which extended the right to counsel in state courts to all indigent defendants in serious criminal cases.[2]

In a lengthy interview a year later, June 26, 1969, Warren elaborated on his view of the Court's proper role. Acknowledging that the Court "makes law," not "consciously," and not "by intending to usurp the role of Congress but because of the very nature of our job," Warren hailed the law made in the reapportionment decisions as the most in-fluential judicial legislation of his tenure; indeed, these cases raised "per-haps the most important issue we have had before the Supreme Court." At stake, Warren thought, was the future of "representative government in this country." "If everyone in this country has an opportunity to participate in his government on equal terms with everyone else and can share in electing representatives who will be truly representative of the entire community and not some special interest, then," the Chief Justice reasoned, "most of these problems that we are now confronted with would be solved through the political process rather than through the courts." Accordingly, the Warren Court had a judicial duty to de-clare that one man's vote should be equal to every other man's vote in the election of state legislators and members of the House of Representatives. Not surprisingly, Warren concluded this interview by expressing the fond hope that history would remember his Court as "the court of the people."[3]

Any affinity between Warren's phrase "the court of the people" and Lincoln's Gettysburg Address was surely intended; after all, the Chief Justice, speaking for a nearly unanimous Court in *Reynolds v. Sims,* twice boldly invoked that famous speech as authority for the one man, one vote doctrine. First he quoted Justice William O. Douglas, who, speaking for the Court, including Warren, in an earlier reapportionment case, had said: "The concept of political equality from the Declaration of Independence to Lincoln's Gettysburg Address, to the Fifteenth, Seventeenth, and Nineteenth Amendments can mean only one thing—one person, one vote."[4] Later, in *Reynolds,* the Chief Justice insisted that the one man, one vote doctrine "is at the heart of Lincoln's vision of 'govern-ment of the people, by the people, [and] for the people.'"[5] Needed, then, was a Court "of the people," a Court dedicated to historic ideals of equality and, moreover, not afraid to exercise independent judicial judgment in their service. For history, the Constitution, and documents having no constitutional relevance rarely spoke ambiguously to the Warren Court; as Justice Douglas aptly put it: "The concept of political equality . . . can mean only one thing. . ."

A sense of urgency also contributed to the Warren Court's quest for egalitarianism in American society. Indeed, a year after his retirement, Warren identified the failure of the nation to live up to its historic ideals of equality as the root cause of the crisis then dividing America. Addressing the NAACP Legal Defense and Educational Fund, Inc., May 15, 1970, he said that there was "a divisiveness in our society to a degree of intensity that has not been equaled in the past hundred years." While many factors contributed to the crisis—among them, "war, inflation, unemployment with resulting poverty; a deterioration of our environment; an atmosphere of repression"—none, Warren believed, was "as basic as our neglect in reaching the ideal we fashioned for ourselves in the Declaration of Independence," namely, the goals of equality and inalienable rights. The other cause, he added, was "our failure to enforce adequately the first section of the 14th Amendment." "If the letter and spirit of these injunctions had been observed everywhere in the United States," Warren concluded, "many of the factors I have just mentioned would be nonexistent today, and those remaining would, in all probability, be manageable."[6]

For Earl Warren, then, equality was an ideal whose realization was long overdue. Dedicated to the Declaration, the Gettysburg Address, and especially to the Bill of Rights, which as early as 1947 he called the "heart of any constitution,"[7] Warren symbolized his Court's commitment to a particular political philosophy, one quite candidly reflected in the Court's leading decisions which sought to bring about equality— in the political process, among the races, and between the rich and the poor, the informed and the uninformed in the administration of criminal justice. Underlying this unmistakable egalitarian impulse was, on one hand, the belief that a democratized, majoritarian political process would enable society to solve its problems there instead of in the courts, and, on the other hand, a remarkable unwillingness to abide even by the outcome of a democratized political process when its results conflicted with the Warren Court's independent judgment.

RACIAL EQUALITY

The era of the Warren Court opened with a decision later considered by the Chief Justice his Court's second most important, *Brown v. Board of Education*, the school desegregation decision of May 17, 1954. Appropriately enough, Justice Jackson, author of the opinion of the Court a decade earlier in the second *Flag Salute* case, set the tone for the Warren Court's approach to *Brown*. During oral argument in 1953, Jackson addressed Assistant Attorney General J. Lee Rankin, arguing for the United States as *amicus* in support of the Negro plaintiffs: "I suppose that realistically the reason this case is here is that action couldn't be obtained from Congress."[8] Indeed, action could not be obtained from Congress. Although explicitly empowered under Section 5 of the Fourteenth Amendment "to enforce, by appropriate legislation," the provisions of the Amendment, including the Equal Protection Clause, Congress had failed to outlaw segregated public schools. Had Congress so acted, its legislation would surely have been constitutional under the reasonable doubt test even in the face of a judicial determination that the history of the Fourteenth Amendment was inconclusive with respect to its intended effect on segregated public schools. For unless the Amendment were intended to exclude such congressional enforcement, an independent congressional judgment that segregated schools violated the Equal Protection Clause would not be unreasonable.

Congress, however, while constitutionally permitted, was not constitutionally required to make such a judgment and to act on it. But the Court was not even permitted under the reasonable doubt test to invalidate segregated public schools because the intended effect of the Fourteenth Amendment on segregated schools was, by the admission of a unanimous Court, inconclusive. Exhaustive examination of the relevant sources did "cast some light," Chief Justice Warren wrote, but "not enough to resolve the problem with which we are faced. At best, they are inconclusive . . . with respect to segregated schools." Yet this judicial finding, at odds with Justice Black's later statements that he joined the opinion because the Thirteenth, Fourteenth, and Fifteenth Amendments, he thought, conclusively barred racial segregation,[9] did not deter the Court; its unanimity was perhaps best explained by Wallace Mendelson's suggestion that "no Justice was prepared to face history with the albatross of racialism upon him."[10] History for the Warren Court in *Brown* proved, as Edmond Cahn has observed, "an element far too ambiguous to be considered very important, much less decisive."[11] Accordingly, the Warren Court refused to "turn the clock back to 1868 when the Amendment was adopted, or even to 1896 when *Plessy v. Ferguson* was written." Instead, the Chief Justice insisted, the Court "must consider public education in the light of its full development and its present place in American life throughout the Nation. *Only in this way* can it be determined if segregation in the public schools deprives these plaintiffs of the equal protection of the laws."[12]

As early as *Brown*, then, Chief Justice Warren had adopted a creative approach to constitutional adjudication. This approach, which involved the exercise of independent judicial judgment in the service of constitutional change, was candidly acknowledged by the Chief Justice a decade later when he joined, with Justice Douglas, in Justice Goldberg's concurring opinion in *Bell v. Maryland* (1964). Arguing that the Equal Protection Clause guaranteed equal access to places of public accommodation, Goldberg urged that "even if the historical evidence were not as convincing as I believe it to be, the logic of *Brown* . . . , based as it was on the fundamental principle of constitutional interpretation proclaimed by Chief Justice Marshall" in *McCulloch,* required the Court to update the Fourteenth Amendment. Although disavowing any judicial duty to "rewrite or amend" the Constitution, Goldberg nevertheless implored the Court in *Bell* to "assess the status of places of public accommodation 'in the light of' their 'full development and . . . present place' in the life of American citizens," just as the Court in *Brown* had considered public education "in the light of its full development and its present place in American life." Goldberg thought that Justice Black's dissent in *Bell,* joined by Justices Harlan and White, ignored "a pervasive principle of constitutional adjudication" and departed from "the ultimate logic of *Brown.*"

Black's dissent had departed from the *Brown* approach, but it had not ignored Marshall's "fundamental principle of constitutional interpretation." Instead Black, who argued that the Equal Protection Clause alone did not bar discrimination in privately owned restaurants, had interpreted Marshall's famous principle correctly:

We are admonished that in deciding this case we should remember that "it is *a constitution* we are expounding." We conclude as we do because we remember that it is a Constitution and that it is our duty "to bow with respectful submission to its provisions." And in recalling that it is a

Constitution "intended to endure for ages to come," we also remember that the Founders wisely provided the means for that endurance: changes in the Constitution, when thought necessary, are to be proposed by Congress or conventions and ratified by the States. The Founders gave no such amending power to this Court.[13]

Two years after *Bell* the *Brown* approach was again explicitly affirmed, this time by Justice Douglas in *Harper v. Virginia* (1966), in which the Court struck down a state poll tax for violating the Equal Protection Clause. Speaking for five other members of the Court including the Chief Justice, Douglas invoked *Brown* as leading precedent for judicial updating of the Fourteenth Amendment. Like Goldberg in *Bell,* Douglas denied any judicial duty to rewrite or amend the Constitution. "Our conclusion," he insisted, "is founded not on what we think governmental policy should be, but on what the Equal Protection Clause requires." But what the Equal Protection Clause required depended on the Court's independent judgment:

[T]he Equal Protection Clause is not shackled to the political theory of a particular era. In determining what lines are unconstitutionally discriminatory, we have never been confined to historic notions of equality, any more than we have restricted due process to a fixed catalogue of what was at a given time deemed to be the limits of fundamental rights. . . . Notions of what constitutes equal treatment for purposes of the Equal Protection Clause *do* change.[14]

Again Black dissented. He accused the majority of exceeding "its limited power to interpret the original meaning of the Equal Protection Clause" by giving that clause "a new meaning" which the Court "believes represents a better governmental policy." The majority had consulted "its own notions," Black charged, on the untenable ground "that to save the country from the original Constitution the Court must have constant power to renew it and keep it abreast of this Court's more enlightening theories of what is best for our society." Repudiating judicial creativity in the service of desirable constitutional change, he claimed that when a political theory embodied in our Constitution becomes outdated, a majority of the Court is "not only without constitutional power" but is "far less qualified to choose a new constitutional political theory" than the electorate proceeding in the manner provided by Article 5.

Justice Black, of course, shared the Court's antagonism toward making payment of a tax a prerequisite to voting, but like the other dissenters,

Justices Harlan and Stewart, he could not conclude that a state poll tax, however unwise, was clearly irrational. The basis for such a tax—the state's desire to collect its revenue and its belief that voters who pay a poll tax will be interested in furthering the state's welfare when they vote—was not unreasonable. "Certainly it is rational to believe," Black thought, "that people may be more likely to pay taxes if payment is a prerequisite to voting." Harlan agreed, and in his dissent, joined by Stewart, he chided the majority for reading out of the Equal Protection Clause a rational discrimination clearly supported by history. After all, Harlan pointed out, property qualifications and poll taxes have been "a traditional part of our political structure"; "it is only by judicial fiat that it can be said, especially in the context of American history, that there can be no rational debate as to their advisability." Yet the Court had attributed to the Equal Protection Clause "the unsupportable proposition" that equal protection "simply means indiscriminate equality." To be sure, Harlan admitted, property and poll tax qualifications "are not in accord with current egalitarian notions of how a modern democracy should be organized." As Douglas had written for the Court, "notions" of equal protection "*do* change." But while it was "entirely fitting that legislatures should modify the law to reflect such changes in popular attitudes," it was "all wrong," Harlan urged, "for the Court to adopt the political doctrines popularly accepted at a particular moment of our history and to declare all others to be irrational and invidious, barring them from the range of choice by reasonably minded people acting through the political process."

Concluding his dissent, Harlan noted that the majority in *Harper* had invoked Justice Holmes's famous warning about the Due Process Clause in *Lochner v. New York* (see Chapter 3). In *Harper,* Douglas, too, reasoned that "the Equal Protection Clause is not shackled to the political theory of a particular era." The analogy, however, was inapt. For in *Lochner* the Court had struck down legislation in the name of a particular economic theory, *laissez-faire,* and Holmes, dissenting, had applied the reasonable doubt test in support of the legislation. But in *Harper* the dissenters, not the majority, used the reasonable doubt test to uphold the poll tax which the majority, exercising independent judgment, invalidated in the name of a particular political theory. With justification, then, Harlan turned Holmes's admonition against the majority in *Harper:* just as the Due Process Clause does not embody the *laissez-faire* philosophy of Herbert Spencer's *Social Statics,* "neither does the Equal

Protection Clause," Harlan observed, "rigidly impose upon America an ideology of unrestrained egalitarianism."

If the Court's reliance in *Harper* on Holmes's dissent in *Lochner* was misplaced, its reliance on *Brown* was not; for the exercise of independent judicial judgment in *Harper,* designed to update the Equal Protection Clause, paralleled the Court's creative approach to *Brown.* Justice Black's defense in *Harper* of his participation in the *Brown* decision, rested, therefore, not on the approach the majority in *Harper,* as well as three justices in *Bell,* attributed to *Brown,* but rather on Black's belief that the Civil War Amendments clearly outlawed state discrimination based on race or color,[15] Chief Justice Warren's contrary opinion for a unanimous Court, including Black, notwithstanding. On the other hand, Justice Harlan's defense of *Brown* in *Harper* is less forthright. Harlan, who succeeded Justice Jackson to the Court and did not participate in the first *Brown* decision, refused to endorse the creative judicial approaches to *Harper* and *Bell,* but he did not endorse Justice Black's support of *Brown* either. Instead, he averred in *Harper* that the Equal Protection Clause, as applied to state discrimination based on race, "*may* embody a particular value in addition to rationality"; its historical intent "*might*" give "racial equality" a "special status."[16] Harlan's reluctant admission that state discrimination based on race might not be subject to the reasonable doubt test, which he praised in *Harper* because that standard "reduces to a minimum the likelihood that the federal judiciary will judge state policies in terms of the individual notions and predilections of its own members," suggests that he might not have concurred either in the first *Brown* decision or in the Chief Justice's opinion.

The demise of the reasonable doubt test under the Warren Court began, therefore, with *Brown v. Board of Education,* in which rationality as the measure of equal protection went the way of history. The Court implicitly recognized what Alexander M. Bickel called "the obvious omission" in the reasonable doubt test—"namely, the question, not whether a legislative choice is rational . . . but whether it is *good.*"[17] An additional judgment to the one required by the reasonable doubt test was often called for; and if the political processes failed to make the "good" choice, the Warren Court was often ready to substitute its independent judgment. When the national political process failed to desegregate the public schools in the District of Columbia and refused to enforce desegregation in twenty-one states,[18] the Court intervened. Scrutinizing "with particular care," Chief Justice Warren noted in *Bolling v. Sharpe,* the District of

Columbia case,[19] classifications based upon race because "they are contrary to our traditions and hence constitutionally suspect," the Court attempted to legitimize, as footnote four had suggested, the claim of a racial minority subject to prejudice and unable to alter the adverse outcome of the political process. More than that, the Warren Court felt a heightened responsibility to exercise independent judgment when the political processes themselves were too clogged, impure, corrupted, undemocratic, or antimajoritarian[20] to achieve "good" results. Such judgment involved not merely a judicial corrective for the "wrong" outcome of the political processes, but stronger, surer medicine: judicial reform of the political system itself.

VOTING RIGHTS

Chief Justice Warren considered the reapportionment decisions, embodying the one man, one vote principle, his Court's most important achievement. If congressional inaction induced the Warren Court to fashion a judicial remedy for the grievance of a racial minority in *Brown,* then congressional failure to reapportion itself equitably and to impose equitable reapportionment upon the state legislatures seems even more likely to have impelled judicial reform of the political processes. As Justice Tom C. Clark indicated in his concurring opinion in *Baker v. Carr,* in which the Court entertained jurisdiction over alleged malapportionment of state legislatures under the Equal Protection Clause of the Fourteenth Amendment: "I would not consider intervention by this Court into so delicate a field if there were any other relief available to the people of Tennessee." Challenging dissenting Justice Frankfurter's faith in the ballot box, Clark asserted that "the majority of the people of Tennessee have no 'practical opportunities for exerting their political weight at the polls'" to correct the existing malapportionment. While conceding that "perhaps" there "may be" recourse in Congress, Clark dismissed that remedy as lacking "substance." "To date," he concluded, "Congress has never undertaken such a task in any State."

Justice Harlan, dissenting, attributed Clark's rationale to the entire majority in *Baker.* "From a reading of the majority and concurring opinions," he thought, "one will not find it difficult to catch the premises that underlie this decision." That the appellants "have been unable to obtain political redress of their asserted grievances appears to be regarded as a matter which should lead the Court to stretch to find some basis for judicial intervention." In *Wesberry v. Sanders,* in which the Court applied the one man, one vote doctrine to the House of Representatives, Harlan again dissented, repeating the charge: "The unstated premise of the Court's conclusion quite obviously is that the Congress has not dealt, and the Court believes it will not deal, with the problem of congressional apportionment in accordance with what the Court believes to be sound political principles."

The unstated premise in *Baker* and *Wesberry* was unmistakably confirmed by Chief Justice Warren himself, speaking for the whole Court except Harlan, in *Reynolds v. Sims,* in which the one man, one vote doctrine was extended to both houses of all state legislatures. "No effective political remedy to obtain relief against the alleged malapportionment," Warren observed, "appears to have been available." "Legislative inaction, coupled with the unavailability of any political or judicial remedy," had yielded a "perpetual scheme" of malapportionment which the Chief Justice called "little more than an irrational anachronism." In short, the political processes having failed to purify themselves, the Warren Court would intervene.

Yet in *Baker* the Court gave no indication that the one man, one vote standard would characterize the purification process. Indeed, Justice Brennan's opinion of the Court, in which he explicitly invoked the traditional test of rationality under the Equal Protection Clause, implied that neither complete nor even approximate equality in the political process was constitutionally required. "Judicial standards under the Equal Protection Clause," he wrote, "are well developed and familiar, and it has been open to the courts since the enactment of the Fourteenth Amendment to determine ... that a discrimination reflects *no* policy, but simply arbitrary and capricious action."[21] Justice Douglas, concurring, agreed: "Universal equality is not the test; there is room for weighting." So did Justice Stewart, also concurring. To him the Court did not "say or imply that state legislatures must be so structured as to reflect with approximate equality the voice of every voter." Nor did the Court "say or imply that there is anything in the Federal Constitution to prevent a State, acting not irrationally, from choosing any electoral legislative structure it thinks best suited to the interests, temper, and customs of its people." The Fourteenth Amendment, Stewart affirmed, "permits the States a wide scope of discretion in enacting laws which affect some groups of citizens differently than others."

Despite these disclaimers in *Baker*,[22] one man, one vote became the judicial remedy for malapportioned state legislatures and for the House of Representatives. Voting equality thereby joined racial equality as a major goal of the Warren Court. Unlike the Court's creative approach in *Brown*, however, where the Chief Justice's opinion eschewed history in favor of updating the Fourteenth Amendment, Justice Black's opinion of the Court in *Wesberry*, consistent with his approval of the result in *Brown*, relied solely on history. "We hold," he announced, "that, construed in its historical context, the command of Article 1, Section 2, that Representatives be chosen 'by the People of the several States' means that as nearly as is practicable one man's vote in a congressional election is to be worth as much as another's." "The debates at the Convention," Black explained, "make at least one fact abundantly clear: that when the delegates agreed that the House should represent 'people' they intended that in allocating Congressmen the number assigned to each State should be determined solely by the number of the State's inhabitants."

History makes that fact abundantly clear, but certainly not the conclusion to which Black blithely jumped: "It would defeat the principle solemnly embodied in the Great Compromise—equal representation in the House for equal numbers of people—for us to hold that, within the States, legislatures may draw the lines of congressional districts in such a way as to give some voters a greater voice in choosing a Congressman than others." For, as Justice Harlan's dissent,[23] which Black completely ignored, and the work of other scholars[24] have effectively demonstrated, history weighed more heavily against the Court's result in *Wesberry* than it did in *Brown*. History being merely inconclusive in *Brown*, the Court through its Chief Justice moved to what Robert G. Dixon, Jr. has called "impregnable higher ground,"[25] the creative approach to constitutional adjudication; but in *Wesberry* the Court through Justice Black rejected the creative approach and simply "mangled constitutional history," as Alfred H. Kelly has put it.[26]

With some justification, perhaps, Chief Justice Warren and not Justice Black wrote for the Court in *Reynolds*. Returning to the *Brown* approach, Warren ignored history—and not without reason; for history would have served the majority no better in *Reynolds* than it had in *Wesberry*. Accordingly, the Chief Justice avoided rather than rebutted the historical scholarship in Justice Harlan's dissent.[27] Warren also conveniently ignored the approach he had taken to the Equal Protection Clause in *McGowan v.*

Maryland (1961). There the Court, speaking through the Chief Justice, upheld the constitutionality of Sunday closing laws. "A statutory discrimination will not be set aside," Warren wrote, "if any state of facts reasonably may be conceived to justify it." Relying specifically on this statement, Harlan, dissenting in *Baker,* expressed incredulity over any suggestion that systems of representation could not rationally include factors other than population. "It is surely beyond argument," he thought, "that those who have the responsibility for devising a system of representation may permissibly consider that factors other than bare numbers should be taken into account."

Neither history nor the reasonable doubt test, however, deterred the Court in *Reynolds.* The *Brown* approach prevailed; indeed, Warren explicitly invoked *Brown* as controlling precedent.[28] Moreover, the Chief Justice implicitly invoked the heart of the political process argument in footnote four of *Carolene Products.* "Especially since the right to exercise the franchise in a free and unimpaired manner is preservative of other basic civil and political rights," Warren reasoned, "any alleged infringement of the right of citizens to vote must be carefully and meticulously scrutinized." Careful scrutiny of alleged malapportionment yielded preferred constitutional status for "the democratic ideals of equality and majority rule," ideals which had "served this Nation so well in the past" and which were "hardly of any less significance for the present and the future." After all, history had witnessed "a continuing expansion of the right of suffrage in this country," Warren noted, citing the Fifteenth, Seventeenth, Nineteenth, Twenty-third, and Twenty-fourth Amendments as well as congressional civil rights legislation of 1957 and 1960. Justice Harlan, the lone dissenter in *Reynolds,* did not overlook the Court's reliance on nonjudicial constitutional change:[29]

If constitutional amendment was the only means by which all men and, later, women, could be guaranteed the right to vote at all, even for *federal* officers, how can it be that the far less obvious right to a particular kind of apportionment of *state* legislatures . . . can be conferred by judicial construction of the Fourteenth Amendment?[30]

Justice Harlan's question answers itself: the Warren Court felt free, perhaps obliged, to exercise independent judicial judgment in the service of preferred freedoms, in this case "the democratic ideals of equality and majority rule." Imposing its own view of how democratic the political process should be, the Court, through its Chief Justice, declared that the "right to vote freely for the candidate of one's choice is of the essence of a democratic society, and any restrictions on that right strike at the heart of representative government." That "the right of suffrage can be denied by a debasement or dilution of the weight of a citizen's vote just as effectively as by wholly prohibiting the free exercise of the franchise" seemed self-evident to the Court. That it begged the question seemed irrelevant, for the Court was committed to a particular political philosophy, what Harlan called "a piece of political ideology." "Logically," Warren reasoned, "in a society ostensibly grounded on representative government, it would seem reasonable that a majority of the people of a State could elect a majority of that State's legislators. To conclude differently, and to sanction minority control of state legislative bodies, would appear to deny majority rights in a way that far surpasses any possible denial of minority rights that might otherwise be thought to result." That less than majoritarian systems of representation might also seem reasonable—"The existence of the United States Senate," Harlan asserted in *Baker*, "is proof enough of that"[31]—was not relevant, much less controlling; for the Court ignored the reasonable doubt test. Through its independent judgment, the Court instead concluded that our "constitutional system amply provides for the protection of minorities by means other than giving them majority control of state legislatures."

The Warren Court's creative approach to constitutional adjudication, begun in *Brown* and extended in the reapportionment decisions, suffered a temporary setback two years after *Reynolds* when, in *Fortson v. Morris* (1966), a sharply divided Court upheld Georgia's system of having the state legislature select a governor from the two persons receiving the highest number of votes in a general election in which no candidate obtained a majority. Justice Black's majority opinion relied on history; the Georgia plan, "as old as the Nation itself," did not violate the Equal Protection Clause. Rejecting judicial updating of the Fourteenth Amendment, Black's opinion, consistent with his approval of *Brown*, his dissents in *Bell* and *Harper*, and his approach in *Wesberry*, drew the wrath of the four dissenters. Justice Douglas, joined by the Chief Justice and Justices Brennan and Fortas, found the Georgia plan antimajoritarian and contrary to the one man, one vote principle. Fortas, joined by Warren and Douglas, objected even more strongly. The Warren Court's "understanding and conception of the rights guaranteed to the people" by the Fourteenth

Amendment, Fortas declared, "have deepened, and have resulted in a series of decisions, enriching the quality of our democracy." *Baker, Gray v. Sanders, Wesberry, Reynolds,* and *Harper* had "reinvigorated our national political life at its roots so that it may continue its growth to realization of the full stature of our constitutional ideal." The *Fortson* decision, Fortas lamented, was "a startling reversal," "a belittling" of the Warren Court's record. By relying on history the Court had mistakenly departed from the method used in *Reynolds;* for history, Fortas urged, was as irrelevant here as it had been in *Reynolds.* Citing Harlan's dissent in *Reynolds,* Fortas allowed that he had "no doubt" that "in the early days of the Nation many of the state legislatures were malapportioned." "Certainly," he emphasized, "the antiquity of the practice did not cause this Court to refrain from invalidating malapportionment under the Equal Protection Clause." In short, the Court had failed in its duty to update the Fourteenth Amendment in the service of majoritarian democracy.

Despite the *Fortson* decision, perhaps "an *ad hoc* aberration," as Bickel observed,[32] the creative approach prevailed. In the last term of the Warren Court the Chief Justice, writing for a majority of seven in *Powell v. McCormack* (1969), upheld the right of Adam Clayton Powell, Jr. to be seated in the Ninetieth Congress. Warren held that the House of Representatives lacked discretionary power to deny membership by a majority vote; the Framers, he determined, clearly intended that Congress could judge only the qualifications expressly set forth in Article 1, Section 5 of the Constitution. Yet the Chief Justice was not content to rely alone on historical intent, however conclusive. He could not resist adding the caveat: "Had the intent of the Framers emerged from these materials with any less clarity, we would nevertheless have been compelled to resolve any ambiguity in favor of a narrow construction of the scope of Congress' power to exclude members-elect." At stake was not just Powell's right to be seated, not just Congress's interest in preserving its institutional integrity, but, apparently of overriding concern, the right of a majority of voters to elect a congressman of their choice. After all, Warren emphasized: "A fundamental principle of our representative democracy is, in Hamilton's words, 'that the people should choose whom they please to govern them.'" Thus, "both the intention of the Framers" and "an examination of the basic principles of our democratic system" persuaded the Warren Court to vindicate Powell's claim. Even where constitutional ambiguity did not exist, the Court, led by its Chief Justice, felt a duty to exercise independent judgment in behalf of a purified political process.

The political process argument reached full bloom under the Warren Court in *Kramer v. Union Free School District* (1969), decided on the same day as the *Powell* case. Without explicitly acknowledging footnote four, the Court, through Chief Justice Warren, clearly relied on its rationale and even its language to strike down under the Equal Protection Clause a section of the New York Education Law which provided that in certain New York school districts residents who are otherwise eligible to vote in state and federal elections may vote in school district elections only if they own or lease taxable real property within the district or are parents or guardians of children enrolled in the local public schools. Referring six times to the need for "more exacting judicial scrutiny" of legislation impairing the purity of the political process, the Court flatly rejected the reasonable doubt test as well as the traditional presumption of constitutionality. In a characteristic display of candor, Chief Justice Warren, speaking for a majority of six, built on paragraphs two and three of footnote four:

[T]he deference usually given to the judgment of legislators does not extend to decisions concerning which resident citizens may participate in the election of legislators and other public officials. Those decisions must be carefully scrutinized by the Court to determine whether each resident citizen has, as far as is possible, an equal voice in the selections. Accordingly, when we are reviewing statutes which deny some residents the right to vote, the general presumption of constitutionality afforded state statutes and the traditional approval given state classifications if the Court can conceive of a "rational basis" for the distinctions made are not applicable. . . . The presumption of constitutionality and the approval given "rational" classifications in other types of enactments are based on an assumption that the institutions of state government are structured so as to represent fairly all the people. However, when the challenge to the statute is in effect a challenge to this basic assumption, the assumption can no longer serve as the basis for presuming constitutionality. And, the assumption is no less under attack because the legislature which decides who may participate at the various levels of political choice is fairly elected. Legislation which delegates decision-making to bodies elected by only a portion of those eligible to vote for the legislature can cause unfair representation. Such legislation can exclude a minority of voters from any choice in the decisions just as effectively as if the decisions were made by legislators the minority had no voice in selecting.

Exercising more exacting judicial scrutiny because the New York statute selectively distributed the franchise in school district elections, the Court held that the classification did not distinguish voters primarily interested in school affairs with sufficient precision to justify denying a voice to Kramer, a nontaxpaying bachelor. Justice Stewart dissented, joined by Justices Black and Harlan, and insisted that the classification clearly related to a legitimate legislative purpose. New York had rationally concluded, Stewart believed, that local educational policy was best left to those persons who had direct and definable interests in that policy, either because they bore the local financial burden or because they were parents of school children. Stewart pointed out that even Justice Douglas, now with the majority, had once observed: "There is no group more interested in the operation and management of the public schools than the taxpayers who support them and the parents whose children attend them."[33] That Kramer might personally be as interested in the conduct of a school district's business as a local taxpayer or parent was no more relevant, the dissenters thought, than the fact that commuters from New Jersey might be as genuinely interested in the outcome of a New York City election as New Yorkers. After all, Stewart wrote, "such discrepancies are the inevitable concomitant of the line-drawing that is essential to lawmaking."

The Court's reliance on the political process argument left the dissenters "at a loss to understand how such reasoning is at all relevant to the present case." In language reminiscent of Justice Frankfurter, dissenting in the second *Flag Salute* case, Stewart pointed out that Kramer was not barred from access to the political process. Eligible to vote in all state, local, and federal elections in which general governmental policy is determined, he was fully able "to participate not only in the processes by which the requirements for school district voting may be changed, but also in those by which the levels of state and federal financial assistance to the District are determined." Kramer clearly was "not locked into any self-perpetuating status of exclusion from the electoral process." Describing Kramer's status as "merely that of a citizen who says he is interested in the affairs of his local public schools," Stewart concluded his dissent by attacking the logical implications of the political process argument itself:

If the Constitution requires that he must be given a decision-making role in the governance of those affairs, then it seems to me that any individual who seeks such a role must be given it. For as I have suggested, there is no persuasive reason for distinguishing constitutionally between the voter qualifications New York has required for its Union Free School District Elections and qualifications based on factors such as age, residence, or literacy.

CRIMINAL JUSTICE

More exacting judicial scrutiny, involving the repudiation of historical intent, the reasonable doubt test, even the presumption of constitutionality, meant also independent judicial judgment in the service of preferred freedoms—equality in the political process, among the races, and, third on Warren's list of major contributions by his Court, in the administration of criminal justice. *Gideon v. Wainwright,* establishing the right to counsel in state courts for indigent defendants accused of serious crimes, took its proper place on the Chief Justice's roll of honor. Decided in 1963 by a unanimous Court, *Gideon* can be viewed as consistent with the Court's traditional approach to the Due Process Clause of the Fourteenth Amendment as espoused by Justice Cardozo in *Palko v. Connecticut* (1937). There the Court expressly affirmed and applied the reasonable doubt test as controlling judicial determination of which Bill of Rights freedoms the Due Process Clause incorporated and to what extent it did so. Construing due process in *Palko* as protecting only those liberties which "have been found to be implicit in the concept of ordered liberty," the Court excluded certain Bill of Rights freedoms precisely because their necessary connection to "the very essence of a scheme of ordered liberty" could not be established beyond a reasonable doubt in 1937. Rights to trial by jury and indictment by grand jury were thus rejected. So too was the immunity from compulsory self-incrimination, for it "might be lost, and justice still done." "Indeed," Cardozo emphasized, citing scholarly authorities to buttress his use of the reasonable doubt test, "today as in the past there are students of our penal system who look upon the immunity as a mischief rather than a benefit, and who would limit its scope, or destroy it altogether." While there would doubtless "remain the need to give protection against torture, physical or mental," it was not "arbitrary or casual"—and therefore not unreasonable—to conclude that justice "would not perish if the accused were subject to a duty to respond to orderly inquiry."

In like fashion Cardozo reasoned that the particular kind of double jeopardy involved in *Palko* did not clearly violate the Due Process Clause. He carefully distinguished the issue, which he left open,[34] whether a state would deny due process if it were permitted "after a trial free from error to try the accused over again or to bring another case against him," from the issue in *Palko:*

The state is not attempting to wear the accused out by a multitude of cases with accumulated trials. It asks no more than this, that the case against him shall go on until there shall be a trial free from the corrosion of legal error. . . . If the trial had been infected with error adverse to the accused, there might have been review at his instance, and as often as necessary to purge the vicious taint.

Connecticut's statute merely involved a "reciprocal privilege" which was not unreasonable. "The edifice of justice stands," Cardozo concluded, "its symmetry, to many, greater than before."

Whether the Court in *Gideon* rejected the reasonable doubt test, so prominent in *Palko,* is uncertain; surely the reasonable doubt test would have yielded the same result.[35] More certain, however, is that in companion cases involving criminal procedure under the Due Process Clause, the Warren Court clearly abandoned the reasonable doubt test in favor of the more creative approach taken in the segregation and reapportionment decisions. Notable for their reliance on independent judicial judgment in behalf of greater egalitarianism in the administration of criminal justice[36] are *Miranda v. Arizona* (1966) and *Duncan v. Louisiana* (1968). Especially revealing are the opinions of Justice White, dissenting in *Miranda* and speaking for the Court in *Duncan,* for they characterize the Warren Court's creative approach to constitutional adjudication and confirm the implications of independent judicial judgment.

Chief Justice Warren, writing for the *Miranda* majority of five, held that state courts could not admit as evidence statements stemming from custodial interrogation of the defendant, unless the state demonstrates the use of procedural safeguards effective to secure the privilege against self-incrimination. In a strident dissent, joined by Justices Stewart and White, Justice Harlan faulted both the constitutional foundation and the desirability of the Court's ruling. "Nothing in the letter or the spirit of the Constitution or in the precedents," he insisted, "squares with the heavy-handed and one-sided action that is so precipitously taken by the Court in the name of fulfilling its constitutional responsibilities."[37] Viewed, moreover, as "a choice based on pure policy," Harlan thought these new rules were "a highly debatable, if not one-sided, appraisal of the competing interests." "I seriously doubt," he added, that "the Court's own finespun conception of fairness" is "shared by many thinking citizens in this country." Reminding the Court, in the words of Cardozo, that "justice, though due to the accused, is due to the accuser also,"[38] Harlan concluded that "the Court has not and cannot make the powerful showing that its new rules are plainly desirable in the context of our society, something which is surely demanded before those rules are engrafted onto the Constitution and imposed on every State and county in the land." In short, the dissenters accused the Court of using independent judicial judgment to justify a result that the reasonable doubt test would not—indeed, could not—yield.

In a separate dissent, joined by Justices Harlan and Stewart, Justice White, who had concurred in Harlan's dissent, approved the majority's creative approach but not the result. White candidly admitted that the Court does—and should—make policy, presumably on the basis of its independent judgment and not the reasonable doubt test; he merely disagreed with the wisdom of the Court's decision, apparently because it did not square with *his* independent judgment. White conceded that the Court's holding is "neither compelled nor even strongly suggested by the language of the Fifth Amendment," is "at odds with American and English legal history," and involves "a departure from a long line of precedent." Nevertheless, he insisted that while the Court's approach "does not prove either that the Court has exceeded its powers or that the Court is wrong or unwise in its present reinterpretation of the Fifth Amendment," the decision does "underscore the obvious":

that the Court has not discovered or found the law in making today's decision, nor has it derived it from some irrefutable sources; what it has done is to make new law and new public policy in much the same way that it has in the course of interpreting other great clauses of the Constitution. This is what the Court historically has done. Indeed, it is what it must do and will continue to do until and unless there is some fundamental change in the constitutional distribution of governmental powers.

At bottom, Justice White seemed to imply that what was good for the Court was good for Justice White also; so long as the majority felt free to exercise independent judgment to create new constitutional law, he was entitled to the same privilege and was prepared to exercise it. Accordingly, Justice White proceeded to exercise independent judgment in *Duncan v. Louisiana*, this time for a majority, and he thereby parted company with Justice Harlan. Holding that the Sixth Amendment right to jury trial in serious criminal cases is fundamental to the American scheme of justice, the Court incorporated the federal guarantee into the Due Process Clause of the Fourteenth Amendment. Despite the acknowledgment of "important dicta" in *Palko* (Cardozo's "weighty and respectable" conclusion that the right to jury trial is not clearly essential to ordered liberty), despite the concession that jury trial has "its weaknesses and the potential for misuse,"[39] despite the citation of professional criticism that raised serious questions about the fundamental fairness of jury trial, and despite the explicit refusal to assert "that every trial—or any particular trial—held before a judge alone is unfair or that a defendant may never be as fairly treated by a judge as he would by a jury," the Court nevertheless rejected the *Palko* approach in favor of independent judicial judgment.

Justice Harlan, joined by Justice Stewart but not Justice White, dissented. Affirming the *Palko* approach, they accused the majority of making "no real analysis" of whether jury trial is "critical to procedural fairness." Examining the available evidence, the dissenters concluded that the "virtues and defects of the jury system have been hotly debated for a long time, and are hotly debated today, without significant change in the lines of argument." Yet the Court had chosen, through its independent judgment, to "impose upon every State one means of trying criminal cases." It is "a good means," the dissenters allowed, "but it is not the only fair means, and it is not demonstratably better than the alternatives States might devise."

If the reasonable doubt test yielded for Justices Harlan and Stewart consistent results in *Duncan* and *Miranda*, independent judgment yielded for Justice White apparently inconsistent results; for the issues in both cases are basically indistinguishable, and jury trial is surely no more—or less—essential to fundamental fairness in criminal due process than the rules mandated in *Miranda*. The implication, of course, is that independent judicial judgment, like reasonable legislative judgment, can often go either way. More importantly, the exercise of independent judicial judgment, permitting, even encouraging, the exercise of judicial choice between constitutionally permissible alternative policies, calls into question the

Hamiltonian justification for judicial review. For if judges will not or cannot be held to the rigors of the reasonable doubt test to reduce judicial bias and policy-making, then Hamilton's warning, written in a defense of judicial review, should be considered. If judges "should be disposed to exercise WILL instead of JUDGMENT," he thought, "the consequence would . . . be the substitution of their pleasure to that of the legislative body. The observation, if it prove anything, would prove that there ought to be no judges independent of that body."[40] To the extent that what Hamilton called "will" may be what Thayer called "independent judgment" and what Hamilton called "judgment" requires application of the "reasonable doubt" test, the Warren Court, like certain of its predecessors, stands indicted.

6

CONCLUSION: CONSTITUTIONAL CHANGE—
Ends and Means

The reasonable doubt test has its limitations. Intended to narrow the scope of judicial judgment to minimize erroneous judicial construction of the Constitution at the expense of reasonable legislative interpretation, it still requires discretion. Like any other guideline, it can be and has been ignored, misapplied, and otherwise abused. But these transgressions do not necessarily indict the guideline, for the reasonable doubt test has often been correctly applied and remains a workable standard in constitutional adjudication. Even Alexander Bickel conceded that "unless one takes a cynical view of the human capacity to reason," the reasonable doubt test "will answer to descriptions of 'correct' or 'erroneous.'"[1]

Yet Bickel, like a growing number of constitutional scholars, insisted that "it has not always been possible to be satisfied that what is rational is constitutional," and that the "real question" may be whether legislation is "good." The answer, he concluded, "may depend on the assignment of preponderant weight to one or another value."[2] Arthur S. Miller and Ronald F. Howell agree. Indeed, they seek to make a virtue of independent judicial judgment. They urge that the search for "true neutrality" in constitutional adjudication is "a bootless quest," that value choices are "inevitable," and therefore that the quest for impartiality in the judicial process be jettisoned in favor of a "result-oriented" jurisprudence, one purposeful in nature rather than "impersonal" or "neutral." Judicial decisions should be evaluated in terms of their "social adequacy" and their realization of "stated societal values," broadly defined by Miller and Howell as "furthering the democratic ideal."[3] Even much-maligned

Herbert Wechsler, whose support of "neutral principles"[4] in constitutional adjudication had triggered Miller and Howell's critique of his thesis, later admitted that the application of neutral principles entailed judicial choice between competing values.[5]

More recently, other students of constitutional law have reached similar conclusions. Gerald Garvey has praised the Warren Court for moving "toward a jurisprudence of concepts tailored to the realities rather than the shadows of American politics"; "wisely and well," he believes, the Court began "to move constitutional interpretation *beyond the Constitution.*"[6] Walter F. Murphy and Joseph Tanenhaus also endorse the new "political jurisprudence," which envisions judges operating as "social engineers," and they regret that "political scientists have made remarkably few efforts to order coherently and then justify a broad set of goals and values that society, *and judges in particular,* should be fostering."[7] Ronald Dworkin concurs. He sharply rebukes lawyers, and by implication all students of public law, for failing to fuse "constitutional law and moral theory" so that observers of the Supreme Court can better evaluate its decisions in terms of the "good"—the "just"—society, and so that the Court, in fashioning wise public policy, can have resort to better moral justifications. The "academic debate," Dworkin charges, "has so far failed to produce an adequate account of where error lies" because the union of constitutional law and moral theory he advocates has yet to occur. But, Dworkin cautiously concludes, "better philosophy is now available."[8]

This developing call for social scientists to help equip the Court to rise above the Constitution, to make "good" public law based on compelling moral theory, raises disturbing problems. "There is, of course," Dworkin himself admits, "a very lively dispute in moral philosophy about the nature and standing of moral rights, and considerable disagreement about what they are, if they are anything at all." Dworkin also concedes that "a theory of political *skepticism,*" involving the propositions that individuals "have only such *legal* rights as the Constitution grants them, and these are limited to the plain and uncontroversial violations of public morality that the framers had actually in mind," would justify a scope for judicial review much narrower than he and others advocate. But he insists that once one grants the existence of moral rights against the state beyond those constitutionally protected, then the reasonable doubt test is an inadequate standard of judicial review. Although Dworkin accepts, even praises, the impartiality argument as the strongest justification for judicial review, and although he confesses that judicial "activism involves risks of tyranny," he nevertheless asserts that the impartiality argument requires judges to exercise a reviewing power broader than the reasonable doubt test, in effect, an independent judgment, in pursuit of the correct moral principles to be incorporated into the Constitution.[9]

Even granting Dworkin's highly debatable assumption that correct moral principles are discoverable, his position is shaky. He admits that those principles have not yet been discovered. That being the case, has not the Court, following Dworkin's own reasoning, been on occasion excessively premature in updating and rewriting the Constitution? Should not the Court have awaited more certain discovery of correct moral principles instead of attempting to foist upon American society values that are, by Dworkin's admission, still uncertified as "morally" good? After all, do we really want the Supreme Court, as Charles P. Curtis once asked, to be the prophet of our natural law?[10]

At bottom, the issue addressed is how constitutional change should occur. The Constitution, of course, clearly provides its own amendment procedure, which, if deemed too difficult, could be formally amended to provide for an easier procedure. Why, then, should the Court act as a continuing constitutional convention? The notion that the Court must be the voice of a "living Constitution," so as better to safeguard liberties thought by some to be incompletely preserved by the Constitution, not only runs into the problem that correct moral principles are elusive; it also permits judicial disregard for constitutional liberties. If the Court, even circumscribed by the reasonable doubt test, has often erred, how much more potential for judicial error exists without that limitation on the scope of judicial judgment?

Like Miller and Howell, like Murphy and Garvey, and like others who urge judicial updating of the Constitution in accordance with correct moral theory, Dworkin advances a position thoroughly at odds with both the impartiality argument for judicial review and the reasonable doubt test. This is an end-justifies-the-means philosophy which suffers not only from the dubious desirability of the means but also from the uncertain morality of the ends. His position admittedly depends on the ability of judges, aided by social scientists, to discover correct moral principles and probably depends on another premise whose truth is not self-evident: that a constitution should require most, if not all, that is "good" and should prohibit most, if not all, that is "bad." Even granting both assumptions, I would urge that correct moral principles, when discovered, find their way into the Constitution through Article 5. Like Curtis, I would leave "our natural law to take its chances without a national prophet."[11]

NOTES

INTRODUCTION

1. Archibald Cox, *The Warren Court: Constitutional Decision as an Instrument of Reform* (Cambridge: Harvard University Press, 1968), pp. 4, 106-7, 22-23.
2. Cox, *The Role of the Supreme Court in American Government* (New York: Oxford University Press, 1976), p. 105.
3. Berger, *Congress v. The Supreme Court* (Cambridge: Harvard University Press, 1969), pp. 343, 346.
4. 7 *Harvard Law Review* 129 (1893).
5. Harlan B. Phillips, ed., *Felix Frankfurter Reminisces* (New York: Reynal and Co., 1960), p. 301.
6. Charles L. Black, Jr., *The People and the Court: Judicial Review in a Democracy* (Englewood Cliffs, N.J.: Prentice-Hall, 1960), p. 193.

1: THE HAMILTONIAN DOCTRINE OF JUDICIAL REVIEW

1. Louis Hartz, *The Liberal Tradition in America* (New York: Harcourt, Brace & World, 1955), pp. 140, 10.
2. Willmoore Kendall, *John Locke and the Doctrine of Majority-Rule* (Urbana: University of Illinois Press, 1965), p. 99.
3. John Locke, *Second Treatise on Civil Government,* in Sir Ernest Barker, ed., *Social Contract* (New York: Oxford University Press, 1962), p. 73. (Emphasis added.)
4. Ibid., pp. 80, 9-10.
5. Ibid., pp. 52, 10. See also p. 9.
6. Ibid., pp. 76, 52-53. See also pp. 80, 84.
7. Ibid., pp. 99, 141, 87. See also pp. 100, 121, 131, 141-42.
8. See ibid., pp. 56-58, for Locke's clearest statement of his doctrine of majority rule. See also p. 104. And see pp. 121, 131, for Locke's requirement that only a majority can rightly rebel.
9. For Locke's view of the fate aggrieved minorities would be likely to suffer under his political system, see ibid., p. 121.
10. Ibid., pp. 142, 99.

11. See especially Raoul Berger, *Congress v. The Supreme Court* (Cambridge: Harvard University Press, 1969). See also Henry M. Hart and Herbert Wechsler, *Federal Courts, and the Federal System* (Brooklyn: Foundation Press, 1953).

12. Max Farrand, ed., *The Records of the Federal Convention of 1787* (New Haven: Yale University Press, 1966), I, pp. 108, 97–98; II, p. 75 (hereinafter cited as Farrand).

13. Ibid., II, pp. 76, 73, 80.

14. Ibid., II, pp. 82, 79; I, p. 98.

15. Ibid., II, pp. 75, 298. See also *The Federalist* (New York: E. P. Dutton & Co., 1948), p. 378 (hereinafter cited as *The Federalist*), where Hamilton in No. 73 summarized the convention's opposition to a council of revision, pointing out that "the judges, who are to be the interpreters of the law, might receive an improper bias, from having given a previous opinion in their revisionary capacities. . . . It is impossible to keep the judges too distinct from every other avocation than that of expounding the laws. It is peculiarly dangerous to place them in a situation to be either corrupted or influenced by the Executive." For Madison's view in favor of a council of revision, see Farrand, I, p. 138.

16. Ibid., II, p. 299.

17. Robert Yates, "Letters of Brutus," in Cecelia M. Kenyon, ed., *The Antifederalists* (Indianapolis: Bobbs-Merrill, 1966), pp. 339, 336.

18. John Bach McMaster and Frederick D. Stone, eds., *Pennsylvania and the Federal Constitution* (The Historical Society of Pennsylvania, 1888), p. 250.

19. Jonathan Elliot, ed., *The Debates in the Several State Conventions on the Adoption of the Federal Constitution* (Washington, D.C., 1836), II, pp. 83, 315, 321, 316 (hereinafter cited as Elliot). (Emphasis in original.)

20. McMaster and Stone, eds., *Pennsylvania and the Federal Constitution*, pp. 297, 343.

21. See, e.g., Farrand, I, p. 60.

22. McMaster and Stone, eds., *Pennsylvania and the Federal Constitution*, p. 394.

23. "When the Almighty himself," Madison remarked, "condescends to address mankind in their own language, his meaning, luminous as it must be, is rendered dim and doubtful by the cloudy medium through which it is communicated." *The Federalist*, No. 37, p. 180.

24. Kenyon, ed., *The Antifederalists*, pp. 342, 335, 338, 351–52, 357. (Emphasis in original.)

25. Edward S. Corwin, *The Doctrine of Judicial Review* (Gloucester, Mass.: Peter Smith, 1963), pp. 63–64; Corwin, *Court over Constitution* (Princeton: Princeton University Press, 1938), p. 68; Corwin, "The Progress of Constitutional Theory Between the Declaration of Independence and the Meeting of the Philadelphia Convention," 30 *American Historical Review* 511, 526 (1925).

26. *The Federalist*, No. 81, p. 412.

27. Ibid., No. 80, p. 407.

28. Ibid., No. 81, p. 412. (Emphasis added.)

29. Ibid., No. 22, p. 108.

30. Ibid., No. 81, p. 413.

31. Ibid., No. 78, pp. 398–99. (Emphasis added.)

32. Madison, James Wilson, and George Mason, leading advocates of a council of revision, clearly understood its defeat to limit judicial review to the constitutionality and not the wisdom of legislation. Farrand, II, pp. 73, 74, 78.

33. *The Federalist*, No. 78, pp. 401, 396, 397, 399. In No. 81, p. 411, Hamilton required "an evident opposition" between the Constitution and the challenged act.

34. Corwin, *Court over Constitution*, p. 66. See also Corwin, *The Doctrine of Judicial Review*, p. 63.

35. Hamilton considered the threat of impeachment a sufficient check. "That is alone a complete security," he remarked in *The Federalist*, No. 81, p. 413.

36. Ronald Dworkin, who considers the impartiality argument implicit in Marshall's justification in *Marbury*, thinks that "the principle that no man should be judge in his own cause" is "so fundamental a part of the idea of legality that John Marshall would have been entitled to disregard it only if the Constitution had expressly denied judicial review." Dworkin, "The Jurisprudence of Richard Nixon," *The New York Review of Books*, May 4, 1972, pp. 31–32.

37. Robert G. McCloskey, *The American Supreme Court* (Chicago: University of Chicago Press, 1960), p. 43.

38. Learned Hand, *The Bill of Rights* (Cambridge: Harvard University Press, 1958), p. 11.

39. James Bradley Thayer, "The Origin and Scope of the American Doctrine of Constitutional Law," 7 *Harvard Law Review* 129, 130 n. 1 (1893). Roscoe Pound, in *The Formative Era of American Law* (Boston: Little, Brown & Co., 1938), pp. 4, 30 n. 2, included Gibson among the ten leading American judges, and Morris R. Cohen in "The Process of Judicial Legislation," 48 *American Law Review* 161, 170 (1914), called him one of the "great creative minds" in American legal history.

40. Because Article 6 imposes the same oath on "Senators and Representatives ... and the Members of the several State Legislatures, and all executive and judicial Officers, both of the United States and of the several states ... ," the oath provision might oblige each of the mentioned officers, in the performance of his own function, to support the Constitution as he alone construes it.

41. See Alpheus T. Mason, *The States Rights Debate: Antifederalism and the Constitution* (Englewood Cliffs, N.J.: Prentice-Hall, 1964); Cecelia M. Kenyon, "Men of Little Faith: The Anti-Federalists on the Nature of Representative Government," 12 *William and Mary Quarterly* 3 (1955).

42. See Hamilton in *The Federalist*, No. 76, p. 389, and Madison in No. 55, p. 286.

43. See especially Berger, *Congress v. The Supreme Court.*

44. *The Federalist*, No. 51, p. 264. (Emphasis added.)

45. Letter from Jefferson to Madison, March 15, 1789, in Julian P. Boyd, ed., *The Papers of Thomas Jefferson* (Princeton: Princeton University Press, 1958) XIV, p. 659. Regarding Jefferson's supposed support of judicial review in this letter, see below, chap. 4, n. 21.

46. *Annals of Congress*, 1st Cong. (1789–90), I, p. 439. (Emphasis added.) At the Philadelphia convention Hugh Williamson of North Carolina had anticipated this argument for a bill of rights. Urging that the Constitution include a prohibition against *ex post facto* laws, Williamson said: "Such a prohibitory clause is in the Constitution of N. Carolina, and tho it has been violated, it has done good there & may do good here, *because the judges can take hold of it.*" Farrand, II, p. 376. (Emphasis added.)

47. Gibson also declared that legislative acts are "in no case to be treated as *ipso facto* void, except where they would produce a revolution in the government."

48. See Madison in *The Federalist*, No. 39, p. 195; No. 43, p. 233; and Hamilton in No. 78, pp. 399–400. See also John Marshall in the Virginia ratifying convention, Elliot, III, p. 554, where the future Chief Justice asked: "What is the service or purpose of a judiciary, but to execute the laws in a peaceable, orderly manner, without shedding blood, or creating a contest, or availing yourselves of force? ... To what quarter will you look for protection from an infringement on the Constitution, if you will not give the power to the judiciary. There is no other body that can afford such a protection."

49. Alpheus T. Mason, *The Supreme Court: Palladium of Freedom* (Ann Arbor: University of Michigan Press, 1962), p. 42.

50. Elsewhere in *Eakin*, Gibson seemed to embrace the doctrine of "departmental construction," declaring that in the few places where the judiciary and not the legislature was the prescribed organ to execute the Constitution, as in the

conduct of trials, the judges were bound to follow the Constitution, a contrary legislative act notwithstanding. He also said a legislative act directing that a court judgment be reversed would be "thought a usurpation of judicial power."
51. Even in this concession Gibson did not address Hamilton's impartiality argument.
52. See, e.g., Paul Brest, *Processes of Constitutional Decisionmaking* Boston: Little, Brown, and Co., 1975), pp. 54–56.
53. Corwin, "The Supreme Court and Unconstitutional Acts of Congress," 4 *University of Michigan Law Review* 616, 625 (1906). (Emphasis in original.)
54. 4 Wheat. 316, 407, 415 (1819). (Emphasis in original.)
55. Alpheus T. Mason and Gerald Garvey, eds., *American Constitutional History: Essays by Edward S. Corwin* (New York: Harper & Row, 1964), pp. 108, 125, 127, 132, 134–35. The literature of American constitutional law truly abounds with mistaken understandings of Marshall's so-called "doctrine of *adaptive* interpretation." Ibid., p. 127. (Emphasis in original.) See, e.g., Robert K. Carr, *The Supreme Court and Judicial Review* (New York: Holt, Rinehart and Winston, 1942), pp. 275–76; Howard E. Dean, *Judicial Review and Democracy* (New York: Random House, 1966), pp. 4, 65, 155, 166; Paul Eidelberg, *The Philosophy of the American Constitution* (New York: The Free Press, 1968), p. 317 n. 32; Arthur S. Miller, *The Supreme Court and American Capitalism* (New York: The Free Press, 1968), pp. 21–24; John E. Nowak, Ronald D. Rotunda, and J. Nelson Young, *Handbook on Constitutional Law* (St. Paul: West Publishing Co., 1978), "1978 Pocket Part," p. 63 n. 134; Arthur E. Sutherland, *Constitutionalism in America* (New York: Blaisdell Publishing Co., 1965), p. 549. Supreme Court Justices have also misinterpreted Marshall's famous dictum. See, e.g., Chief Justice Hughes's opinion of the Court in *Home Building & Loan Association v. Blaisdell,* 290 U.S. 398, 442 (1934); Justice Cardozo's unpublished opinion in *Blaisdell,* reprinted in Alpheus T. Mason and William M. Beaney, eds., *American Constitutional Law* (Englewood Cliffs, N.J.: Prentice-Hall, 1978), p. 393; Chief Justice Vinson's dissenting opinion in *Youngstown v. Sawyer,* 343 U.S. 579, 682 (1952); Justice Brennan's concurring opinion in *Abington School District v. Schempp,* 374 U.S. 203, 230, 241 (1963); Justice Goldberg's concurring opinion in *Bell v. Maryland,* 378 U.S. 226, 312 (1964); Justice Blackmun's separate opinion in *Regents of the University of California v. Bakke,* 57 L Ed 2d 750, 844–45 (1978).
56. 4 Wheat. 316, 402. (Emphasis added.) Earlier judicial formulations of the reasonable doubt test appear in Justice Iredell's opinion in *Calder v. Bull,* 3 Dall. 386, 399 (1798), and in Justice Chase's opinion in the same case, p. 395. See also Chief Justice Marshall's opinion of the Court in *Fletcher v. Peck,* 6 Cranch 87, 123 (1810). Some delegates to the Philadelphia convention, notably George Mason of Virginia and Gouverneur Morris of Pennsylvania, expressed similar thoughts. Farrand, II, pp. 78, 299. See also Iredell's reply to Richard Spaight of North Carolina, quoted in Berger, *Government by Judiciary: The Transformation of the Fourteenth Amendment* (Cambridge: Harvard University Press, 1977), p. 309 n. 39. And, of course, see Hamilton, *The Federalist,* No. 78, pp. 396–97; No. 80, p. 407; No. 81, pp. 411–12. See as well James Bradley Thayer's discussion of the origins of the reasonable doubt test in "The Origin and Scope of the American Doctrine of Constitutional Law," pp. 140–42.
57. Ibid., pp. 415–16. (Emphasis added.)
58. When his opinion in *Eakin v. Raub* was cited in argument in *Norris v. Clymer,* 2 Penna. 281 (1845), Gibson, then Chief Justice of the Pennsylvania Supreme Court, replied to counsel: "I have changed that opinion, for two reasons. The late convention [which framed the Pennsylvania Constitution of 1838], by their silence, sanctioned the pretensions of the courts to deal freely with Acts of the Legislature; and from experience of the necessity of the case." Once converted, Gibson exercised the judicial veto more than once. See Stanley I. Kutler, "John Bannister Gibson:

Judicial Restraint and the 'Positive State,'" 14 *Journal of Public Law* 181 (1965). Learned Hand's reluctant acceptance of judicial review is also based on "the necessity of the case." Hand, *The Bill of Rights*, pp. 11, 14, 15, 29.

59. N. C. Phillips, "Political Philosophy and Political Fact: The Evidence of John Locke," in *Liberty and Learning: Essays in Honor of Sir James Hight* (Christchurch, N.Z.: Whitcombe and Tombs, 1950), p. 208.

60. In the Virginia ratifying convention Marshall seems to have recognized the impartiality argument. Elliot, III, pp. 552, 559.

2: JAMES BRADLEY THAYER AND JUDICIAL JUDGMENT

1. 7 *Harvard Law Review* 129 (1893) (hereinafter cited as "Origin and Scope").

2. Harlan B. Phillips, ed., *Felix Frankfurter Reminisces* (New York: Reynal and Co., 1960), pp. 299–301. See also Frankfurter's tribute to Thayer in *West Virginia v. Barnette*, 319 U.S. 624, 667 (1943), and Holmes's letter to Thayer, in which Holmes agreed "heartily" with his essay. Quoted in Mark De Wolfe Howe's introduction to *James Bradley Thayer, Oliver Wendell Holmes, and Felix Frankfurter on John Marshall* (Chicago: University of Chicago Press, 1967), p. xi (hereinafter cited as *Thayer, Holmes, and Frankfurter on Marshall*).

3. Charles L. Black, Jr., *The People and the Court: Judicial Review in a Democracy* (Englewood Cliffs, N.J.: Prentice-Hall, 1960), pp. 203–4.

4. Ibid., pp. 205–10. See also Paul Eidelberg, *The Philosophy of the American Constitution* (New York: The Free Press, 1968), pp. 312 n. 4, 314 n. 20; Richard Harris, "Taking the Fifth," *The New Yorker*, April 12, 1976, p. 68.

5. Black, *The People and the Court*, p. 205. See also Martin Shapiro, *Freedom of Speech: The Supreme Court and Judicial Review* (Englewood Cliffs, N.J.: Prentice-Hall, 1966), p. 16; Howard E. Dean, *Judicial Review and Democracy* (New York: Random House, 1966), pp. 114–15.

6. Eugene V. Rostow, *The Sovereign Prerogative: The Supreme Court and the Quest for Law* (New Haven: Yale University Press, 1962), pp. 30 n. 39, 179.

7. Felix S. Cohen, "Transcendental Nonsense and the Functional Approach," in L. K. Cohen, ed., *The Legal Conscience—Selected Papers of Felix S. Cohen* (New Haven: Yale University Press, 1960), p. 44.

8. Alexander M. Bickel, *The Least Dangerous Branch: The Supreme Court at the Bar of Politics* (New York: Bobbs-Merrill Co., 1962), pp. 42–43; Bickel, *Politics and the Warren Court* (New York: Harper & Row, 1965), pp. 177–81.

9. Shapiro, *Freedom of Speech*, p. 115. Shapiro labels the doctrine as one of "preferred positions."

10. Black, *The People and the Court*, pp. 198–99; Dean, *Judicial Review and Democracy*, pp. 116–18· Robert G. McCloskey, "The Scope of Judicial Review," in McCloskey, ed., *Essays in Constitutional Law* (New York: Vintage Books, 1957), p. 60.

11. Black, pp. 199, 214–15; Dean, p. 168.

12. "Origin and Scope," p. 130 n. 1.

13. Thayer, "John Marshall," in *Thayer, Holmes, and Frankfurter on Marshall*, pp. 77, 80. Thayer expressed the same opinion in his 1893 essay: "The reasoning was simple and narrow. Such was Hamilton's method in the Federalist. . . . As the matter was put, the conclusions were necessary." "Origin and Scope," pp. 138–39. See also p. 130, where Thayer asserted that the constitutional text did not "necessarily" imply judicial review.

14. "Origin and Scope," p. 139.

15. Ibid., p. 140.

16. Ibid., p. 138. (Emphasis added.)

17. Ibid., pp. 138, 150. (Emphasis in original.) For a recent statement of the argument Thayer here rejected, see Black, *The People and the Court*, p. 204.

18. Ibid., pp. 143–44. (Emphasis added.)
19. Thayer, "Constitutionality of Legislation: The Precise Question for a Court," Letter to the Editor, 38 *The Nation* 314–15 (1884).
20. "Origin and Scope," pp. 152, 145.
21. Ibid., pp. 138, 152. (Emphasis added.) See also p. 136, where Thayer opined that judicial review was not regarded by the Framers "as the chief protection against legislative violation of the constitution."
22. Ibid., pp. 135–37. See also Thayer, *Legal Essays* (Boston: The Boston Book Co., 1908), p. 9 n. 1, where he quoted with approval the Massachusetts court in *Kendall v. Kingston*, 5 Mass. 524, 533 (1809): The legislature "must, in the first instance, but not exclusively, be the judge of its powers, or it could not act." See also Donald G. Morgan, *Congress and the Constitution: A Study of Responsibility* (Cambridge: Harvard University Press, 1966), for some of the implications of congressional failure to consider carefully the constitutionality of its legislation. Charles Black, however, denies that the oath legislators take to support the Constitution implies any necessary judicial respect for legislative judgment (*The People and the Court*, p. 214).
23. "Origin and Scope," p. 147.
24. Thayer, *A Preliminary Treatise on Evidence at the Common Law* (Boston: Little, Brown and Co., 1898), pp. 208–9. At p. 210 n. 2, Thayer added: "This distinction is of fundamental importance in constitutional law, where courts are reviewing the action of legislatures and considering whether they have kept within the limits of legislative power." See also Thayer, *Cases on Constitutional Law* (Cambridge: George H. Kent, 1895), I, p. 672.
25. "Origin and Scope," p. 150 (Emphasis in original).
26. Ibid., p. 151.
27. Thayer, *A Preliminary Treatise on Evidence at the Common Law*, p. 210.
28. "Origin and Scope," p. 151. (Emphasis added.)
29. Ibid., p. 144. Cooley's remark is quoted in Thayer, *Cases on Constitutional Law*, I, pp. 172–75.
30. Ibid., pp. 137–38. (Emphasis added.) At pp. 140–41, Thayer cited James Wilson's identical observation, made in the Philadelphia convention, that laws might be dangerous and destructive, yet not so "unconstitutional as to justify the judges in refusing to give them effect."
31. Ibid., p. 141. See also Chief Justice Richardson's opinion in *Dartmouth College v. Woodward*, 1 New Hampshire 11, 115 (1817): "If we refuse to execute an act warranted by the constitution, our decision in effect alters that instrument and imposes new restraints upon the legislative power which the people never intended."
32. Ibid., pp. 145–46.
33. Ibid., pp. 146, 151, 149.
34. Thayer, "John Marshall," in *Thayer, Holmes, and Frankfurter on Marshall*, p. 88.
35. As Alexander M. Bickel has rightly observed, "it does not take a lunatic legislature to enact measures that are irrational." Bickel invoked *Wieman v. Updegraff*, 344 U.S. 183 (1952), as a classic example of a clearly unconstitutional state act. *The Least Dangerous Branch*, pp. 39–42. See also "Origin and Scope," p. 134, for examples cited by Thayer of clearly unconstitutional acts.
36. See, e.g., Chief Justice Waite's statement for the Court in *Munn v. Illinois*, 94 U.S. 113, 132 (1877): "For our purposes we must assume that, if a state of facts could exist that would justify such legislation, it actually did exist when the statute now under consideration was passed."
37. "Origin and Scope," pp. 146, 138, 148.
38. See ibid., p. 149, where Thayer, referring to such constitutional freedoms as the prohibition against *ex post facto* laws and "the provisions about double jeopardy, or giving evidence against one's self, or attainder, or jury trial," clearly indicated that the reasonable doubt test applies to all constitutional freedoms alike.

There is not, I believe, the slightest suggestion in his writings supporting the doctrine of preferred freedoms.

39. Curiously, Learned Hand's approach to the problem of conflicting constitutional values required judges to inquire whether the legislative accommodation was impartially reached. See Hand, *The Bill of Rights* (Cambridge: Harvard University Press, 1958), pp. 65–66. See also Irving Dilliard, ed., *The Spirit of Liberty: Papers and Addresses of Learned Hand* (New York: Vintage Books, 1959), pp. 211–12.

40. Thayer, *Legal Essays*, p. 30 n. 2. See also "Origin and Scope," p. 148, where Thayer noted that the reasonable doubt test applies to a potential conflict between power and right: "The judicial function is merely that of fixing the outside border of reasonable legislative action, the boundary beyond which the taxing power, the power of eminent domain, police power, and legislative power in general, cannot go without violating the prohibitions of the constitution or crossing the line of its grants."

41. See "Origin and Scope," pp. 155–56; Thayer, "John Marshall," in *Thayer, Holmes, and Frankfurter on Marshall*, pp. 87–88.

42. Thayer, *Legal Essays*, pp. 30 n. 2, 60.

43. Ibid., p. 152. (Emphasis added.) See also Thayer, "John Marshall," in *Thayer, Holmes, and Frankfurter on Marshall*, p. 78.

44. "Origin and Scope," pp. 154–55. (Emphasis added.)

45. See above, note 10.

46. Thayer's qualifying language supports this interpretation; so does his own application of the rule of administration. See also Justice Frankfurter's dissent in *West Virginia v. Barnette*, 319 U.S. 624, 629 (1943), where Frankfurter rebuked the Court for exercising what he thought was independent judicial judgment to strike down state legislation in the absence of a collision with national power. At pp. 661–62, 666–67, Frankfurter expressly invoked the reasonable doubt test in his attempt to save the legislation. At p. 650, he asserted that "since the First Amendment has been read into the Fourteenth, our problem is precisely the same as it would be if we had before us an Act of Congress for the District of Columbia." At p. 667, Frankfurter again defended application of the reasonable doubt test because the state act did not conflict with the exercise of national power: "Moreover, it is to be borne in mind that in a question like this we are not passing on the proper distribution of political power as between the states and the central government. We are not discharging the basic function of this Court as the mediator of powers within the federal system. To strike down a law like this is to deny a power to all government." See also Frankfurter's opinion of the Court in *Minersville v. Gobitis*, 310 U.S. 586, 598 (1940), overruled by *Barnette*, where he also rejected independent judicial judgment. In a letter of May 27, 1940, to Justice Stone, the lone dissenter in *Minersville*, Frankfurter added: "We are not exercising any independent judgment; we are sitting in judgment upon the judgment of the legislature." Quoted in Alpheus T. Mason, *Security Through Freedom* (Ithaca, N.Y.: Cornell University Press, 1955), p. 218. See also Justice Holmes's classic dissent in *Lochner v. New York*, 198 U.S. 45, 76 (1905), another famous case involving the constitutionality of a state statute in the absence of a clash with national power, where Holmes expressly applied the reasonable doubt test in support of the act.

47. At p. 145 of "Origin and Scope," Thayer invoked Marshall's statement that "in no doubtful case would [the Court] pronounce a legislative Act to be contrary to the Constitution."

48. Ibid., p. 142 n. 1.

49. Ibid., p. 148 n. 1.

50. Ibid., p. 148. Thayer, in approving the *Minnesota Rate* cases, insisted on application of the reasonable doubt test, which more than preserves the presumption of constitutionality in favor of challenged legislation. See also ibid., p. 148 n. 3, which further confirms that Thayer rejected arbitrary judicial definitions of "reasonableness." It should also be noted that Chief Justice Waite, considered by

many a paragon of judicial restraint for his opinion in *Munn v. Illinois,* 94 U.S. 113 (1877), elsewhere expressed views on the substantive limits of state power to regulate public utilities which are remarkably similar to those expressed by Thayer in the quoted passage. In the *Railroad Commission* cases, 116 U.S. 307, 331 (1886), Waite said: "[I]t is not to be inferred that this power of limitation or regulation is itself without limit. This power to regulate is not a power to destroy, and limitation is not the equivalent of confiscation. Under pretence of regulating fares and freights, the State cannot require a railroad corporation to carry persons or property without reward; neither can it do that which in law amounts to a taking of private property for public use without just compensation, or without due process of law."

51. Thayer, *Legal Essays,* p. 36 n. 1. Thayer's exception in the last sentence of this passage should not be interpreted to mean that courts, applying the reasonable doubt test, can overturn congressional judgment on the issue of uniformity, for Thayer had earlier indicated that they cannot. Instead, the reasonable doubt test would properly invalidate congressional legislation if Congress, for example, under the guise of "uniformly regulating commerce," clearly violated constitutionally protected rights. Charles Black, *The People and the Court,* pp. 205–7, presents many examples of far-fetched but possible legislative violations of the Constitution accomplished by labeling constitutionally proscribed legislation as exercises of expressly granted powers. He might also have listed the commerce power as providing a pretense for the exertion of unconstitutional power. Whereas Black believes that such palpable violations of constitutional rights as he hypothesizes could not be checked by Thayer's reasonable doubt test, I disagree.

52. Thayer, *Legal Essays,* p. 36 n. 1. Interestingly, Justice Frankfurter, who accepted Thayer's exception to the rule of administration when federalism was involved (see n. 46 above), departed from Thayer's restriction on that exception. Whereas Thayer limited the exercise of independent judicial judgment to cases where state action allegedly collided with the exercise of national power and precluded any judicial judgment on the need for uniformity when Congress had not acted under its commerce power, Frankfurter, as well as a majority of the modern Court, felt free to exercise independent judgment to strike down state interference with the national commerce power in the absence of congressional regulation. Justice Black, however, adhered strictly to Thayer's view on this subject. See, e.g., *Southern Pacific Co. v. Arizona,* 325 U.S. 761 (1945); *Dean Milk Co. v. Madison,* 340 U.S. 349 (1951). See also Frankfurter, *The Commerce Clause under Marshall, Taney and Waite* (Chicago: Quadrangle Books, 1964).

53. Thayer, *Legal Essays,* p. 36 n. 1. In the same passage Thayer repeated his insistence that "the courts should abstain from interference, except in cases so clear that the legislature cannot legitimately supersede their determinations; for the fact that the legislature may do this, in any given case, shows plainly that the question is legislative, and not judicial." Thayer added: "It is also to be remembered that much in State action, which may not be reached by the courts under the present head [commerce], may yet be controlled by them under other parts of the Constitution, as in such cases as *Crandall v. Nevada* and *Corfield v. Coryell.*" (Citations omitted.) One must assume that Thayer intended the reasonable doubt test to apply to judicial review of state action allegedly in conflict with these "other parts of the Constitution."

54. See Thayer, *Legal Essays,* p. 30 n. 2, where Thayer counseled: "Where our system intrusts a general subject to the legislature, nothing but the plainest constitutional provisions of restraint, and the plainest errors, will justify a court in disregarding the action of its co-ordinate legislative department,—no political theories as to the nature of our system of government will suffice, no party predilections, no fears as to the consequences of legislative action. In dealing with such questions the judges are, indeed, not acting as statesmen, but their function necessarily requires that they take account of the purposes of statesmen and their duties;

for their own question relates to what may be permissible to a statesman when he is required by the Constitution to act, and, in order that he may act, to interpret the Constitution for himself; it is never, in such cases, merely the dry question of what the judges themselves may think that the Constitution means."
55. Ibid., p. 36 n. 1. Congress, as the primary judge of conflict, could not, of course, permit a state to exercise an exclusively national power or to exercise a power in violation of other parts of the Constitution. The issue of conflict under the Supremacy Clause here under discussion—whether state power conflicts with the exercise of national power, not whether state action collides with other constitutional restrictions—arises only if state action does *not* collide with other constitutional restrictions. Thus, in *McCulloch*, where Maryland attempted to exercise, in Thayer's language, one of "its most undoubted powers," that of taxation, the issue of conflict with national power was clearly raised; for in the absence of a conflict with national power, the state tax would have been constitutional. For judicial resolution of the issue of conflict, Thayer would apply the independent judgment test in the service of national supremacy. I would apply the reasonable doubt test. By *either* test the tax, I believe, would fall. For another view, see Fred Rodell, *Nine Men: A Political History of the Supreme Court of the United States from 1790 to 1955* (New York: Vintage Books, 1964), pp. 98–99. Rodell argues that a state tax must be destructive of a national institution in order, under the Supremacy Clause, to be "contrary" to national law and therefore unconstitutional. He thinks that Marshall should have made the "sensible recognition that, whereas some taxes may 'destroy,' others may not." I suggest that a state tax need not be destructive of a national institution in order to be "contrary" to it or in conflict with its operation; an impairment, short of destruction, will do, even under the reasonable doubt test, especially if Congress, the primary judge of conflict, reasonably thinks so.

3: ECONOMIC DUE PROCESS AND THE COMMERCE CLAUSE

1. The term was coined by Edward S. Corwin. See Corwin, "The Passing of Dual Federalism," in Robert G. McCloskey, ed., *Essays in Constitutional Law* (New York: Vintage Books, 1957), pp. 185, 188–89.
2. Alpheus T. Mason and William M. Beaney, eds., *American Constitutional Law* (Englewood Cliffs, N.J.: Prentice-Hall, 1978), p. 357.
3. Charles M. Hough, "Due Process of Law—Today," 32 *Harvard Law Review* 218, 228 (1919).
4. McCloskey, "The Scope of Judicial Review," in McCloskey, ed., *Essays in Constitutional Law*, p. 60.
5. See above, chap. 2, n. 50.
6. 123 U.S. 623, 661, 662, 664 (1887).
7. 134 U.S. 418, 459 (1890). (Emphasis added.)
8. Ibid., pp. 465–66.
9. McCloskey, "Foreword: The Reapportionment Case," 76 *Harvard Law Review* 54, 67–68 (1962). For another view of *Lochner*, see Albert A. Mavrinac, "From *Lochner* to *Brown v. Topeka:* The Court and Conflicting Concepts of the Political Process," 52 *American Political Science Review* 641 (1958).
10. 9 Wheat. 1, 194–95 (1824). Numerous scholars and judges have deemed this an authoritative definition, consonant with the intent of the Framers. See, e.g., Robert L. Stern, "That Commerce Which Concerns More States Than One," 47 *Harvard Law Review* 1335 (1934); Edward S. Corwin, *The Commerce Power versus States Rights* (Gloucester, Mass.: Peter Smith, 1962); Felix Frankfurter, *The Commerce Clause under Marshall, Taney, and Waite* (Chapel Hill: University of North Carolina Press, 1937); Walton H. Hamilton and Douglass Adair, *The Power to*

Govern (New York: Norton, 1937); Paul R. Benson, Jr., *The Supreme Court and the Commerce Clause, 1937-1970* (Cambridge, Mass.: Dunellen, 1970).

11. See also *Standard Oil Co. v. United States,* 221 U.S. 1 (1911), and *United States v. American Tobacco Co.,* 221 U.S. 106 (1911).

12. 247 U.S. 251, 275 (1918).

13. Corwin, "The Anti-Trust Acts and the Constitution," 18 *Virginia Law Review* 1, 361 (1932). (Emphasis in original.)

14. 285 U.S. 262, 284 n. 6 (1932). In note 6, Brandeis also quoted with approval from the *Sinking Fund* cases, 99 U.S. 700, 718 (1879): "Every possible presumption is in favor of the validity of a statute, and this continues until the contrary is shown beyond a reasonable doubt. One branch of the government cannot encroach on the domain of another without danger. The safety of our institutions depends in no small degree on a strict observance of this salutary rule." In notes 6 and 7, Brandeis also cited numerous other cases affirming the reasonable doubt test.

15. 291 U.S. 502, 538 (1934). In a rare example of open judicial willingness, even desire, to contravene this venerable principle of constitutional interpretation, dissenting Justice McReynolds, speaking also for Justices Van Devanter, Sutherland, and Butler, retorted: "But plainly, I think, this Court must have regard to the wisdom of the enactment" (ibid., p. 556).

16. *Home Building and Loan Association v. Blaisdell,* 290 U.S. 398 (1934) was also seen as a good omen for the New Deal.

17. Hughes's position on the scope of Congress's commerce power and on the nature of our federal system was clearly stated seven years earlier in his *The Supreme Court of the United States* (New York: Columbia University Press, 1928), pp. 95-96, 299-300.

18. To support his conclusion that only states, not the national government, could regulate such a local activity as the live-poultry industry, Hughes relied for controlling precedent on *Brown v. Houston,* 114 U.S. 622 (1885). Yet in that case the Court ruled that coal shipped to Louisiana was subject to state taxation but only in the absence of congressional action, whereas the very issue in *Schechter* was the constitutionality of congressional action.

19. See also Robert L. Stern, "The Commerce Clause and the National Economy, 1933-1946," 59 *Harvard Law Review* 645, 660-61 (1946). At p. 651 Stern reasoned: "There would appear to be no difference in the constitutional power to protect interstate commerce against unduly high prices, as in the Sherman Act, and excessively low prices, as in the New Deal legislation."

20. In his concurring opinion in *Schechter,* Cardozo, joined by Stone, explicitly adhered to the direct-indirect effects test and paid deference to "our federal system." 295 U.S. 495, 554. Brandeis wrote no separate opinion.

21. Counsel for the Government had argued: Where "there is a plainly expressed federal power on the one side, and nothing on the other side but the mere general fact that we have a dual form of government, then the controlling consideration of where the line should be drawn seems to be the express language of the Constitution as to where it *is* drawn, rather than what to one mind or another might seem to be the proper distribution of powers which *ought* to prevail on the basis of a general conception and theory of dualism. To adopt the latter test, . . . is, after all, to appeal from the express constitutional provision itself to considerations of policy and to make those considerations the test of constitutional distribution of powers rather than the language of the grant" (ibid., pp. 258-59). (Emphasis in original.)

22. The danger, of course, *was* clearly perceived and the Constitution *was* ratified. See especially Alpheus T. Mason, *The States Rights Debate: Antifederalism and the Constitution* (Englewood Cliffs, N.J.: Prentice-Hall, 1964). See also n. 10 above.

23. *United States v. Butler,* 297 U.S. 1 (1936), had, of course, intervened between *Schechter* and *Carter* and had prompted a scathing dissent written by Justice Stone and joined by Justices Brandeis and Cardozo. Perhaps *Butler* foreshadowed the division of the Court in *Carter*. Justice Roberts's opinion of the Court in *Butler* was a classic example of poorly disguised judicial policy-making. First, Roberts (p. 62) described "the function of this Court" as a simple, mechanical job—"to lay the article of the Constitution which is invoked beside the statute which is challenged and to decide whether the latter squares with the former." Next, at p. 67, he affirmed the reasonable doubt test. Then, after adopting, at pp. 65-66, the Hamiltonian construction of the national taxing power, which was "limited only by the requirement that it shall be exercised to provide for the general welfare of the United States," Roberts proceeded to deny the exercise of that power by, in effect, reading the word "expressly" into the Tenth Amendment. "The act," he wrote, at p. 68, "invades the reserved rights of the states. It is a statutory plan to regulate and control agricultural production, a matter beyond the powers delegated to the federal government." The Tenth Amendment, he added, dictated this conclusion. No power "to regulate agricultural production is given, and therefore legislation by Congress for that purpose is forbidden."

24. Whether Hughes actually switched between *Carter* and *Jones & Laughlin* has been the subject of continuing controversy. His authorized biographer, Merlo J. Pusey, claims that the Chief Justice was quite consistent, that he always adhered to "the distinction between direct and indirect effects upon interstate commerce," and that "the vast differences between the situations" accounted for the change in decisions. See Pusey, *Charles Evans Hughes* (New York: Macmillan, 1951), II, pp. 766-72. Samuel Hendel, *Charles Evans Hughes and the Supreme Court* (New York: Columbia University Press, 1951), pp. 258-69, concurs with Pusey. Alpheus T. Mason, *The Supreme Court: Palladium of Freedom* (Ann Arbor: University of Michigan Press, 1962), pp. 116-48, disagrees, as does Robert L. Stern, "The Commerce Clause and the National Economy, 1933-1946," pp. 680-82.

25. Of the four cases only *Adkins* and *Dagenhart* were expressly overruled.

4: FOOTNOTE FOUR AND PREFERRED FREEDOMS

1. As Learned Hand remarked in 1946: "Just why property itself was not a 'personal right' nobody took the time to explain." Irving Dilliard, ed., *The Spirit of Liberty: Papers and Addresses of Learned Hand* (New York: Vintage Books, 1959), p. 156. See also Hand, *The Bill of Rights* (Cambridge: Harvard University Press, 1958) and Felix Frankfurter, "John Marshall and the Judicial Function," in *James Bradley Thayer, Oliver Wendell Holmes, and Felix Frankfurter on John Marshall* (Chicago: University of Chicago Press, 1967), pp. 159-60. For a thoughtful critique of "the doubtful distinction between economic and civil rights," see Robert G. McCloskey, "Economic Due Process and the Supreme Court: An Exhumation and Reburial," in Philip B. Kurland, ed., *The Supreme Court and the Constitution* (Chicago: University of Chicago Press, 1960), pp. 158-86.

2. Robert H. Jackson, soon to join the Court, observed in 1941: "The presumption of validity which attaches in general to legislative acts is *frankly reversed* in the case of interferences with free speech and free assembly, and for a perfectly cogent reason. Ordinarily, legislation whose basis in economic wisdom is uncertain can be redressed by the processes of the ballot box or the pressures of opinion. But when the channels of opinion and of peaceful persuasion are corrupted or clogged, these political correctives can no longer be relied on, and the democratic system is threatened at its most vital point. In that event the Court, by intervening, restores the processes of democratic government; it does not disrupt them." Jackson, *The Struggle for Judicial Supremacy* (New York: Vintage Books, 1941), p. 285. (Emphasis added.)

3. Chief Justice Stone introduced this expression in *Jones v. Opelika*, 316 U.S. 584, 600, 608 (1942); Justice Douglas invoked it for the majority in *Murdock v. Pennsylvania*, 319 U.S. 105, 115 (1943). For a bitter attack on the idea of preferred freedoms, see Justice Frankfurter's concurring opinion in *Kovacs v. Cooper*, 336 U.S. 77, 90–97 (1949).

4. See, e.g., George D. Braden, "The Search for Objectivity in Constitutional Law," 57 *Yale Law Journal* 571, 580 n. 28 (1948), where the author calls *Stromberg* and *Lovell* "only vaguely relevant" to paragraph one of footnote four.

5. Stone did *not* rely on Cardozo's opinion of the Court in *Palko v. Connecticut*, 302 U.S. 319, 325–28 (1937), where Cardozo asserted that a theory of preferred freedoms was mandated by the Due Process Clause of the Fourteenth Amendment. Significantly, Cardozo did not support reversing the presumption of constitutionality; rather, he believed that the reasonable doubt test controlled judicial judgment.

6. Overruled by *Brandenburg v. Ohio*, 395 U.S. 444 (1969).

7. 4 Wheat. 316, 435–36 (1819).

8. See, e.g., Alpheus T. Mason, "Judicial Activism: Old and New," 55 *Virginia Law Review* 385, 403-4 (1969); Louis Lusky, "Minority Rights and the Public Interest," 52 *Yale Law Journal* 1 (1942); Letter from Stone to Chief Justice Hughes, April 19, 1938, quoted in Mason, *The Supreme Court: Palladium of Freedom* (Ann Arbor: University of Michigan Press, 1962), p. 155.

9. At the end of paragraph three, Stone cited his own opinion of the Court in *South Carolina Highway Dept. v. Barnwell Bros.*, 303 U.S. 177, 184–85 n. 2 (1938), in which the Court struck down state legislation affecting interstate commerce on the ground that "when the regulation is of such a character that its burden falls principally upon those without the state, legislative action is not likely to be subjected to those political restraints which are normally exerted on legislation where it affects adversely some interest within the state." Yet political restraint—action by Congress—was available; that it was not (yet) forthcoming did not necessarily justify a judicial "remedy." See also Stone's similar statements in *McGoldrick v. Berwind-White Coal Mining Co.*, 309 U.S. 33, 46 n. 2 (1940); *Helvering v. Gerhardt*, 304 U.S. 405, 416 (1938); *Southern Pacific Co. v. Arizona*, 325 U.S. 761, 769 (1945); and Justice Black's vehement dissent in the *Southern Pacific* case, pp. 789, 792, 794–95.

10. See, e.g., Mason, "Judicial Activism: Old and New," p. 394; Archibald Cox, *The Warren Court: Constitutional Decision as an Instrument of Reform* (Cambridge: Harvard University Press, 1968), pp. 94–95.

11. Mason, *Security Through Freedom* (Ithaca: Cornell University Press, 1955), p. 127.

12. Lusky, "Minority Rights and the Public Interest," pp. 20–21.

13. See above, chap. 2, n. 55.

14. Elbridge Gerry used the phrase in the Philadelphia convention. Max Farrand, ed., *The Records of the Federal Convention of 1787* (New Haven: Yale University Press, 1966), I, p. 48.

15. See, e.g., Robert A. Dahl, *A Preface to Democratic Theory* (Chicago: University of Chicago Press, 1956); Edward S. Corwin, "The Progress of Constitutional Theory Between the Declaration of Independence and the Meeting of the Philadelphia Convention," 30 *American Historical Review* 511 (1925); Mason, *The States Rights Debate* (Englewood Cliffs, N.J.: Prentice-Hall, 1964); Mason, *The Supreme Court: Palladium of Freedom*.

16. Braden, "The Search for Objectivity in Constitutional Law," p. 580 n. 28.

17. See, e.g., Alexander M. Bickel's perceptive analysis in *The Supreme Court and the Idea of Progress* (New York: Harper and Row, 1970), pp. 36–37, 108–15, 166–73.

18. See, e.g., Braden, "The Search for Objectivity in Constitutional Law," p. 581; Walter F. Murphy, "Deeds Under a Doctrine: Civil Liberties in the 1963 Term," 59 *American Political Science Review* 64, 72–74 (1965).

19. Dahl, *A Preface to Democratic Theory*. See also Bickel, *The Supreme Court and the Idea of Progress*, pp. 36–37.

20. See, e.g., Lusky, "Minority Rights and the Public Interest," pp. 20–21; Mason, "Understanding the Warren Court: Judicial Self-Restraint and Judicial Duty," pp. 560–61; Edmond Cahn, "Supreme Court and Supreme Law: An American Contribution," in Lenore L. Cahn, ed., *Confronting Injustice: The Edmond Cahn Reader* (Boston: Little, Brown & Co., 1966), p. 78.

21. Opposing legislative supremacy in Virginia, Jefferson called for "the proper remedy; which is a convention to fix the constitution, ... to bind up the several branches of government by certain laws, which, when they transgress, their acts shall become nullities; to render unnecessary an appeal to the people, or in other words a rebellion, on every infraction of their rights, on the peril that their acquiescence shall be construed into an intention to surrender those rights." H. A. Washington, ed., *The Writings of Thomas Jefferson* (Washington, D.C.: Taylor and Maury, 1854), VIII, pp. 371–72. Often interpreted as an argument for judicial review, this passage nowhere mentions that institutional innovation. During the struggle over ratification of the Constitution, Jefferson did, of course, alert Madison to an argument in favor of a bill of rights that had "great weight" with Jefferson: "the legal check which it puts into the hands of the judiciary." But even this supposed endorsement of judicial review is hedged by Jefferson's next sentence: "This is a body, which if rendered independent, and *kept strictly to their own department* merits great confidence for their learning and integrity." Letter from Jefferson to Madison, in Julian P. Boyd, ed., *The Papers of Thomas Jefferson* (Princeton, N.J.: Princeton University Press, 1958), XIV, p. 659. (Emphasis added.) The qualifier seems much more consistent with Jefferson's later defense of "departmental construction" of the Constitution than with support of judicial review. Furthermore, when Madison, apparently persuaded by Jefferson concerning the need for a bill of rights, proposed the Bill of Rights amendments to the House of Representatives in 1789, Madison noted that judicial review would be limited to the protection of "rights *expressly* stipulated for ... by the declaration of rights." *Annals of Congress*, 1st Cong. (1789–90), I, p. 439. (Emphasis added.)

22. Letter from Frankfurter to Stone, May 27, 1940, reprinted in Mason, *Security Through Freedom*, p. 218.

23. Jackson, *The Struggle for Judicial Supremacy*, p. 285.

24. See Frankfurter's concurring opinion in *Dennis v. United States*, 341 U.S. 494, 526–27 (1951). Stone, too, may have regretted the footnote. See his letter to Irving Brant, August 25, 1945, quoted in Mason, "Judicial Activism: Old and New," p. 425. Jackson, once a leading defender of footnote four, also expressed doubts. See Jackson, *The Supreme Court in the American System of Government* (New York: Harper and Row, 1955), pp. 57–58, 80–82, as well as his dissent in *Brinegar v. United States*, 338 U.S. 160, 180 (1949).

5: THE WARREN COURT AND INDEPENDENT JUDGMENT

1. Letter from Wyzanski to Alpheus T. Mason, January 22, 1967, quoted in Mason, "Judicial Activism: Old and New," 55 *Virginia Law Review* 385, 424 (1969).

2. *New York Times*, July 6, 1968, p. 1 col. 8.

3. Ibid., June 27, 1969, pp. 1 col. 5, 17 col. 4.

4. 377 U.S. 533, 558 (1964), citing Justice Douglas in *Gray v. Sanders*, 372 U.S. 368, 381 (1963). See also Douglas's dissent, joined by Warren, in *Fortson v. Morris*, 385 U.S. 231, 240 (1966), where the same statement is also cited.

5. Ibid., p. 568. (Brackets in original.)

6. *New York Times*, May 16, 1970, pp. 1 col. 7, 5 col. 4.

7. Governor Earl Warren, *Address to the Legislative Joint Interim Committee on Constitutional Revision and Its Advisory Committee*, Santa Barbara, California,

October 29, 1947, in Henry M. Christman, ed., *The Public Papers of Chief Justice Earl Warren* (New York: Capricorn Books, 1966), p. 7.
8.   22 *U.S. Law Week* 3161 (1953).
9.   See Black's dissent in *Harper v. Virginia*, 383 U.S. 663, 678 n. 7 (1966), and his CBS News Special Broadcast of December 3, 1968, printed in "Justice Black and the Bill of Rights" (New York: CBS, Inc., 1968), p. 4.
10.   Wallace Mendelson, *Justices Black and Frankfurter: Conflict in the Court* (Chicago: University of Chicago Press, 1961), p. 76. See also Richard Kluger's account of the Court's progress toward unanimity in *Brown* in *Simple Justice* (New York: Alfred A. Knopf, 1976).
11.   Edmond Cahn, "A Dangerous Myth in the School Segregation Cases," 30 *New York University Law Review* 150, 152 (1955).
12.   Emphasis added.
13.   Emphasis in original. See also Black, *A Constitutional Faith* (New York: Albert A. Knopf, 1969), pp. 8-14, 21, 35.
14.   Emphasis in original.
15.   383 U.S. 663, 678 n. 7 (1966).
16.   Ibid., p. 682 n. 3. (Emphasis added.)
17.   Bickel, *Politics and the Warren Court* (New York: Harper and Row, 1965), p. 179. (Emphasis in original.)
18.   By 1954 seventeen states and the District of Columbia required segregation in the public schools and four states permitted segregation at the option of local school districts. *Bolling v. Sharpe*, 347 U.S. 497, 500 (1954).
19.   Because it was "unthinkable," at least to the Warren Court in 1954, that what the states could not do Congress could do, the Justices in *Bolling v. Sharpe* performed the remarkable feat, as Walter F. Murphy has quipped, of "incorporat[ing] the Fourteenth Amendment's equal protection clause into the Bill of Rights." Murphy, "Deeds Under a Doctrine: Civil Liberties in the 1963 Term," 59 *American Political Science Review* 64, 78 (1965).
20.   These terms have been used by various writers to describe, however imprecisely, the nature of the political process the Warren Court tried to reform. See, e.g., Archibald Cox, *The Warren Court: Constitutional Decision as an Instrument of Reform* (Cambridge: Harvard University Press, 1968), p. 22; Bickel, *The Supreme Court and the Idea of Progress* (New York: Harper & Row, 1970), p. 32.
21.   Emphasis in original.
22.   Numerous scholars have also read *Baker* as not implying the one man, one vote standard. See, e.g., Robert G. McCloskey, "Foreword: The Reapportionment Case," 76 *Harvard Law Review* 54, 71 (1962); Phil C. Neal, "Baker v. Carr: Politics in Search of Law," in Philip B. Kurland, ed., *The Supreme Court and the Constitution* (Chicago: University of Chicago Press, 1965), p. 187; Martin Shapiro, *Law and Politics in the Supreme Court: New Approaches to Political Jurisprudence* (New York: The Free Press, 1964), p. 242; Cox, *The Warren Court*, p. 117. On the other hand, Justice Frankfurter's dissent in *Baker*, p. 300, asserts that the Court would ultimately require, "if not the assurance of equal weight to every voter's vote, at least the basic conception that representation ought to be reasonably proportionate to population." Justice Harlan's dissent, p. 333, draws the same inference.
23.   Even Justice Clark in his concurring and dissenting opinion in *Wesberry*, p. 18, agreed that Harlan "clearly demonstrated that both the historical background and language preclude a finding that Art. I, sec. 2, lays down the *ipse dixit* 'one person, one vote' in congressional elections."
24.   See, e.g., Alfred H. Kelly, "Clio and the Court: An Illicit Love Affair," in Kurland, ed., *1965 Supreme Court Review* (Chicago: University of Chicago Press, 1965), p. 119; McCloskey, "Foreword: The Reapportionment Case," p. 54; Robert G. Dixon, Jr., *Democratic Representation: Reapportionment in Law and Politics* (New York: Oxford University Press, 1968); Shapiro, *Law and Politics in the Supreme Court*.

25. Dixon, *Democratic Representation*, p. 230.
26. Kelly, "Clio and the Court: An Illicit Love Affair," p. 135.
27. See also Frankfurter's dissent in *Baker*, pp. 301–24; John P. Frank and Robert F. Munro, "The Original Understanding of 'Equal Protection of the Laws,'" 50 *Columbia Law Review* 131 (1950); Dixon, *Democratic Representation*, pp. 277–89; McCloskey, "Foreword: The Reapportionment Case," p. 71.
28. 377 U.S. 533, 566 (1964).
29. Warren also relied on documents having no constitutional relevance – the Declaration of Independence and Lincoln's Gettysburg Address. Ibid., pp. 558, 568.
30. Emphasis in original.
31. See also Harlan's dissent in *Gray v. Sanders*, 372 U.S. 368, 387–88 (1963).
32. Bickel, *The Supreme Court and the Idea of Progress*, p. 111.
33. Douglas made the statement in his dissent in *Doremus v. Board of Education*, 342 U.S. 429, 435 (1952).
34. See Harlan's dissent in *Benton v. Maryland*, 395 U.S. 784, 808 (1969), which overruled *Palko*.
35. See, e.g., Harlan's concurring opinion in *Gideon*, 372 U.S. 335, 352 (1963); Jerold H. Israel, "Gideon v. Wainwright: The 'Art' of Overruling," in Kurland, ed., *The Supreme Court and the Constitution*, p. 263; Anthony Lewis, *Gideon's Trumpet* (New York: Vintage Books, 1964), pp. 173–81.
36. Cox, *The Warren Court*, p. 86, agrees that egalitarianism is the common thread joining the leading decisions of the Warren Court in the areas of segregation, reapportionment, and criminal justice.
37. See also ibid., p. 84.
38. Cardozo made the statement in *Snyder v. Massachusetts*, 291 U.S. 97, 122 (1934).
39. Quoting *Singer v. United States*, 380 U.S. 24, 35 (1965).
40. *The Federalist* (New York: E.P. Dutton & Co., 1948), No. 78, p. 399.

CONCLUSION: CONSTITUTIONAL CHANGE

1. Bickel, *The Least Dangerous Branch* (New York: Bobbs-Merrill, 1962), p. 41.
2. Ibid., p. 39.
3. Miller and Howell, "The Myth of Neutrality in Constitutional Adjudication," 27 *University of Chicago Law Review* 661, 683, 671, 684, 691, 689 (1960).
4. Wechsler, "Toward Neutral Principles of Constitutional Law," 73 *Harvard Law Review* 1 (1959).
5. Wechsler, *Principles, Politics and Fundamental Law* (Cambridge: Harvard University Press, 1961), pp. xiii–xiv. Wechsler's original position appears to be identical. See "Toward Neutral Principles of Constitutional Law," pp. 15, 20.
6. Garvey, *Constitutional Bricolage* (Princeton, N.J.: Princeton University Press, 1971), p. 156. (Emphasis added.)
7. Murphy and Tanenhaus, *The Study of Public Law* (New York: Random House, 1972), pp. 222–23. (Emphasis added.)
8. Dworkin, "The Jurisprudence of Richard Nixon," *The New York Review of Books*, May 4, 1972, pp. 34–35. Dworkin calls John Rawls's *Theory of Justice* (Cambridge: Harvard University Press, 1971) a work that "no constitutional lawyer will be able to ignore."
9. Ibid., pp. 29–32. (Emphasis in original.)
10. Curtis, *Law as Large as Life: A Natural Law for Today and the Supreme Court as Its Prophet* (New York: Simon and Schuster, 1959), p. 102.
11. Ibid., p. 103.